A HOT planet needs cool kids

understanding climate change
and what you can do about it

by Julie Hall

illustrated by Sarah Lane

Green Goat Books

Library of Congress Cataloging-in-Publication Data available.

ISBN 978-0-615-15585-2

Manufactured in Canada.

Design by Sarah Lane.

10 9 8 7 6 5 4 3 2 1

Green Goat Books
P.O. Box 11256
Bainbridge Island, WA 98110

www.greengoatbooks.com

www.progressivekid.com

100% post-consumer
Printed on recycled paper.

For my daughter Lucy

Contents

> *It is not the strongest of the species that survives, nor the most intelligent, but the one most responsive to change.*
> —Charles Darwin

> *We do not inherit the land from our ancestors; we borrow it from our children.*
> —American Proverb

Introduction

Calling Cool Kids!

The fact that you are reading this book means you are already a cool kid. That's a great start, because our hot world needs your help to be cool. Earth is getting too warm too fast, and this sudden change is threatening life on our planet. Climate change, or global warming, is putting all living things in danger—from pine trees to polar bears, coral to cattails, sea lions to salmon, porcupines to people.

There always have been changes in Earth's climate, but the sudden climate change happening right now is the result of things people are doing. People are causing the problem, and people need to solve it. To help prevent further climate change, we need to change the way we live.

As a young person, you are used to change because you do it all the time. Growing up is all about change. You change grades and schools, you change teachers and friends, you change what you know and what you think. Change can be hard and even scary but also exciting. Change can teach you things about life and about yourself that you would never know otherwise.

This book is about change: changes that are happening on Earth and changes that people need to make. You need to change, and you need to help your family and friends change. As the great humanitarian leader Gandhi wisely said, "Be the change you wish to see in the world." This book will tell you why and how. And ideally it will inspire you to get started right away.

Calling Cool Parents!

Although this book can be used by individual kids, parents are encouraged to read it with their kids and together discuss the issues and ideas presented here. Since climate change is affecting and will continue to affect everyone, it is important for the whole family to understand what's at stake and get involved in making lifestyle changes for the entire household.

Many of the activities invite your participation and are a perfect starting point for further investigation and discussion. Although this book is meant to teach kids and inspire them to take action, because the subject matter is at best complex and at worst distressing, guidance and input from parents are highly recommended. The aim of this book is to tell the truth and do it with hope. Your truthfulness and hope will be a powerful resource and model for your child as we all face the challenges and opportunities for growth that lie ahead.

In addition to reading this book and taking action to fight climate change, it is just as important to develop in your child a love for the natural world. Common sense as well as a growing body of research indicate that connection with nature makes kids healthier, happier, and more confident. Moreover, people need to feel personally connected—to care deeply—about something to want to fight to protect it. *Nature-deficit disorder,* a term coined by esteemed nature writer and child advocate Richard Louv, is a condition unique to our time that sadly captures the situation of many children today, leading to obesity, depression, anxiety, violence, and disengagement from life itself.

Take every opportunity to teach and model respect, wonder, and love for all life forms. Talk about what you appreciate about nature. Share experiences in the outdoors or wilderness that inspired you. Spend time with your child outside. Visit parks, forest preserves, beaches, and botanical gardens. Take walks. Volunteer with your child at a wildlife shelter. Go camping. Read about plants and animals. Create animal habitat in your yard or a local park. Plant a garden. Plant trees. Encourage your child to notice the living world around you. If children experience real connections with trees, animals, flowers, fish, wind, water, and soil, they will want to protect them.

Calling Cool Teachers!

Why You Should Teach Your Students About Climate Change

Climate change affects and will continue to affect every aspect of life on Earth. It is the most compelling issue of our time, and it has tremendous importance in the lives of children, since they are the inheritors of what was wrought by those before them. Teaching students about climate change empowers them with knowledge and helps impel them to act—something we all need to do right now if the earth is to remain a habitable place. Climate change is also a highly relevant, real-world subject for conveying vital science and social studies concepts.

Using This Book in the Classroom

This book is designed to be used in the classroom. The many activities (see Contents on pages 4–5) throughout cover science and social studies as well as language arts, art, and mathematics. Look for the school icon accompanying each activity (Action) to find teaching suggestions. In addition to the activities, the Hot Facts, Cool Facts, Eco-Hero features, Chapter Summaries, Terms list, and Resources are effective teaching aids. Chapter objectives, assessments, lesson plans, and national standards correlations are available at http://www.greengoatbooks.com.

Using This Book to Teach Science and Social Studies

The subject of climate change is not just for science classrooms. Climate change is as much about society, business, politics, and ethics as it is about science, and truly understanding it demands looking at life from all of these perspectives. Science and social studies teachers will find this book to be an excellent tool for teaching students the socio-scientific causes and effects of climate change, as well as important science and social studies concepts. This book meets the National Science Education Standards and the National Council for the Social Studies Curriculum Standards. Teachers will find science and social studies standards lists and assessment tools for each chapter of this book at http://www.greengoatbooks.com/HotPlanet.

Cross-Curricular Teaching

In addition to being suitable for science and social studies classrooms, this book works well for cross-curricular teaching. Language arts, mathematics, and art teachers will find appropriate activities throughout the book. For more information about using this book for cross-curricular teaching, visit http://www.greengoatbooks.com.

Age Level

This book can be used for teaching a wide range of ages, from the later elementary through the middle and early high school years.

Clear, accessible language, hands-on activities, and engaging illustrations help communicate complex science and social studies topics in ways that upper elementary students can understand. Elementary school teachers can use this book to introduce climate change concepts and actively involve their students in working to reduce carbon dioxide emissions at school and at home.

Middle school and high school teachers can use the book as the basis for a unit on climate change or as a supplement to teaching science or social studies issues related to climate change. Particularly for older students, Hot Facts, Cool Facts, Eco-Heroes Features, and abundant real-world activities throughout the book provide excellent launch points for further learning, research, and discussion. The book is also a tool for organizing student-driven climate change actions at school or in the community.

A Note of Hope

There is no denying that climate change is a scary thing. In fact, denying that it is is unwise, because denial breeds complacency and inaction. Climate change and our response to it must be taken very seriously by everyone if we hope to ensure that our planet continues to be a habitable place. But it is equally important to instill a sense of hope and positivity in students. If students come to believe that the problems are too big, that the state of the earth is too far gone, they will become numb and paralyzed. We all need to believe there is a future to fight for and that our actions matter.

Perhaps most importantly, young people need to learn to love the earth and its life forms in order to want to fight to save them. One of the best things you can do as a teacher is to teach and model respect, wonder, and appreciation for the natural world, for all living things, and for outdoor experiences beyond the borders of walls and cities. Talk about what you appreciate about nature. Share experiences in the outdoors or wilderness that inspired or changed you. Invite others to visit the class to share their outdoor experiences and knowledge. Take your students outside. Visit a park, forest preserve, botanical garden, or wildlife shelter. Encourage them to notice the living world around them. If students experience real connections with trees, animals, flowers, fish, wind, water, and soil, they will want to learn more about them and protect them.

9

1 What Is Climate Change?

HOT fact

Current climate change is sometimes referred to as anthropogenic climate change because **anthropogenic** means "human-caused."

A lot of people are talking about **climate change** these days. People also call it **global warming**. Maybe you know what it is or have an idea of what it is. Or maybe you don't know about it at all.

This book will help you understand climate change—what is causing it and how it is affecting life on Earth. It also will show you what people are doing to fight climate change and how you can help.

Defining Climate Change

The **climate change** currently happening on Earth is the result of warmer temperatures caused by humans. These wamer temperatures are changing our planet's weather and making conditions more difficult for living things. People are releasing too much carbon dioxide into Earth's atmosphere, which is trapping more heat from the sun and heating up our world.

Wind is one part of climate.

What Is Climate?

Weather changes from hour to hour, day to day, and season to season. **Climate** is what the weather is usually like over long periods of time. The climate in the Midwestern part of the United States, for example, is cold, snowy, and windy in winter. On some winter days the *weather* may be calm, sunny, and warm, but the *climate* is not.

action: What Is the Climate Where You Live?

Look in an almanac or on the Internet to find out the average temperatures, precipitation, and wind patterns where you live. Compare them to the averages in other areas. Then write a sentence describing the climate where you live.

Students work in teams to create sentences. Then they compare their sentences and revise them until they create a consensus sentence about the climate in their area.

Earth's relationship to the sun has a powerful influence on our planet's climate. The earth's movement around the sun creates the four seasons. The sun also affects the earth's temperature and **precipitation** (rain and snow). These elements of Earth's climate interact with each other to affect air and ocean currents around the globe.

The elements of Earth's climate are interrelated, which means that everything interacts with and affects everything else. Ocean currents in Australia, for example, affect the weather in Spain.

Climate includes precipitation, or rain, snow, and hail.

Earth's position relative to the sun

Earth

affects temperature + precipitation

which affect ocean currents + air currents

which affect temperature + precipitation

Global ocean currents move in a giant loop that helps keep the earth's climate stable, or consistent over time. This loop is called the **thermohaline circulation.** It is sometimes called the ocean conveyor belt.

Warm ocean currents move from the earth's warm equator regions (those closest to the sun) to the cold poles (those farthest from the sun).

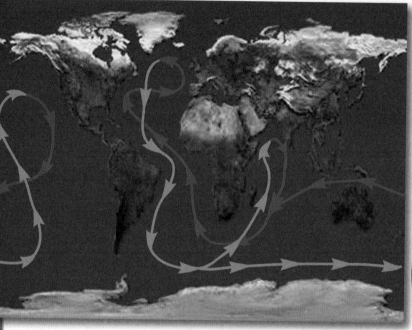

Left: Warm (red) and cold (blue) ocean currents in the thermohaline circulation. Right: satellite image of ocean currents.

Thermohaline Circulation

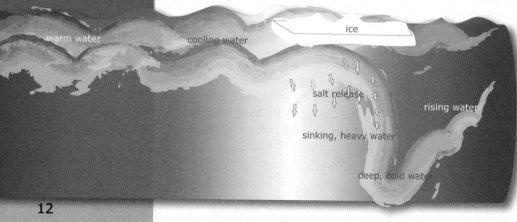

warm water | cooling water | ice | salt release | sinking, heavy water | rising water | deep, cold water

As these warm waters cool off and turn to ice, they release salt. The salt falls to the cold water below the new ice and makes the water heavy. This cold, salty water is so heavy it sinks rapidly—as fast as 5 billion gallons a second. The deep, cold water then continues moving along its loop

NASA's Aquarius project is designed to measure ocean salt levels (salinity) from satellites in space. The redder areas in this image show higher salinity.

the earth's oceans and lead to dramatic climate changes in parts of the world like Europe. Steadily decreasing salt levels in the North Atlantic Ocean in the last 40 years may indicate that the thermohaline circulation is already slowing down.

Climate and Environment

throughout the earth's oceans, mixing with warmer water and rising; then mixing with colder water and falling again.

As ocean waters circulate, they bring **oxygen** to the deep seas and nutrients to shallow waters. They also help to balance temperatures on land. Some scientists believe that climate change could cause the thermohaline circulation to slow down or even stop. This could threaten marine life throughout

Climate affects the environment. It makes it possible for certain kinds of plants and animals to survive and not others. Plants and animals in the Northwestern United States, for example, like moist air and soil and mild temperatures (neither very cold nor very hot). If the climate in the Northwest were to change suddenly from wet and mild to dry and hot or to cold and snowy, much of the animal and plant life there would die.

HOT fact

Some scientists believe that the thermohaline circulation has stopped before, leading to major global climate changes. It may have stopped most recently about 13,000 years ago, bringing about ice-age conditions that lasted for about 12 centuries.

action: Heavy Water

Cold water is heavier than warm water. So is salty water. See for yourself by coloring two cups of warm water with food coloring. Pour cold water into half of the colored water and watch what happens. Then pour salt water into the other cup of colored water and watch what happens.

Students work in pairs to do the experiments. Then each pair creates a chart of the results. As a class, students discuss how their findings help explain the thermohaline circulation. Then they discuss the implications of generally warmer waters.

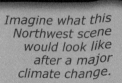

Imagine what this Northwest scene would look like after a major climate change.

13

Earth's Climate

Earth's climate has gone through many changes over time. Volcanoes have erupted, earthquakes have rumbled, asteroids have hit, and ice ages have brought vast sheets of ice called **glaciers** to parts of the earth. Such events have shaped and reshaped the land and sea and changed the earth's environment in dramatic ways.

Changes in Earth's climate have caused some living things to die away. Others have survived through **adaptation** over time. Depending on the type of environment, some characteristics, or traits, allowed certain members of a **species** to survive, while other characteristics did not.

Through **genetic** changes over many generations, living things become adapted to their environments, each with a unique climate: **temperate** and **tropical** rainforests, **arid** deserts, snowy mountains, grassy plains, warm shallow seas, and deep cold oceans, to name a few.

How Scientists Study Climate

Much of what scientists know about Earth's climate over the last hundred thousand years comes from studying ice cores in central Greenland drilled 2 miles deep. Because snow is different in summer and winter, scientists can date each seasonal layer of ice like rings of a tree. They study each ice layer to find out annual summer and winter temperatures.

Scientists once believed that Earth's climate could change only very slowly over long periods of time. But by studying the ice cores they have discovered that Earth's climate can experience sudden dramatic shifts. For example, after a period of rapid warming about 13,000 years ago Earth's temperatures suddenly dropped back into ice-age conditions. They remained cold for about 12 centuries before suddenly warming up again.

During this period of sudden temperature change, many large animals, or **megafauna,** that lived on Earth at the time

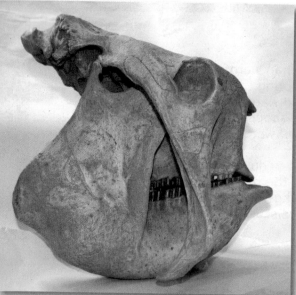

Skull of a glyptodon, a giant, armadillo-like mammal that became extinct 10,000 years ago. Glyptodons were as big as a small car.

became extinct. These extinctions included species such as the mammoth, giant sloth, giant beaver, giant deer, dire wolf, sabre-tooth cat, wooly rhinoceros, giant snake, meat-eating kangaroo, cave bear, giant duck, and giant condor. Stress from climate change, along with overhunting by human cultures like the Clovis people, are possible causes of the extinctions. Up to 70 percent of people may have died off as well in some areas.

Many scientists believe that this sudden ice age, called the Younger Dryas, happened because the thermohaline circulation stopped. Others suggest that the Younger Dryas was brought on by a comet striking North America.

Giant sloths could weigh 13,000 pounds. Some were taller than the largest mammoth.

Human-Made Climate Change

There always will be natural climate changes on Earth. But the kind of climate change we discuss in this book is happening because of things people have done and are doing. These changes are taking place very quickly, making the earth warmer than it used to be when you were born. If climate change continues at its current rate, it will be hotter by the end of this century than it has been for two million years.

It might sound good to have warmer weather, like more time to be outside and grow things in the garden. But having our climate, or normal weather conditions, shift suddenly is dangerous for all living things, including people.

action: The Goldilocks Planet

Imagine the first living thing in our galaxy is looking for a home planet. Draw a picture showing why it would choose Earth. What would it think about other planets in our galaxy? What would it like about Earth?

Students choose a medium for representing Earth as a good planet choice: an illustration, a story, a play, a poem, a song. Then students share their creations in a presentation called Celebrate Earth: Why Our Planet Makes the Best Home.

Chapter Summary

Climate is what the weather is like over long time periods. Earth's climate changes naturally, but the kind of climate change discussed in this book is caused by people. Earth's relationship to the sun strongly affects our climate, influencing temperature, precipitation, and air and ocean currents. The elements of Earth's climate are interrelated: Changes to one part affect other parts. Earth's climate and environment also are interrelated. Climate shapes the environment and life forms. Human-made climate change is changing our environment and making life much harder for all living things.

2 How Climate Change Is Changing Our World

I hope they never get a rope on you, weather.
I hope they never put a bit in your mouth.
I hope they never pack your snorts
into an engine or make you wear wheels.
—May Swenson, "Weather"

Earth is getting warmer very quickly. Warmer temperatures are changing rain, snow, and wind patterns all over the world. These changes are affecting ocean currents, which in turn also affect temperature, precipitation, and wind conditions. Sudden changes to these climate relationships are disturbing the balance of Earth's climate that has existed for thousands of years. As this balance is being lost, the weather in many places is becoming more extreme.

The Weather Is Changing

Some areas of Earth are getting more rain that usual, causing flooding. Very cold places with snow and glaciers also are having flooding because of melting ice. Melting glaciers are starting to raise sea levels. Some islands and low-lying coastal areas are washing away with rising water.

Other places on Earth are having very dry weather, bringing drought and fires. Some lakes and rivers have become smaller or dried up, leaving little or no water for people and animals and for farming. Soil is drying up in some places, too, leading to erosion and poor farming conditions.

Many scientists also believe that climate change is creating more powerful storms than in the past. They expect that areas used to storms will have stronger ones, and places that don't normally have certain kinds of storms will start to have them. Have you noticed the weather changing where you live? If so, how?

Melting Ice and Snow

Melting sea ice is shrinking and breaking apart in places like the Arctic, Antarctica, and Greenland, stranding wildlife such as polar bears, seals, walruses, and penguins out at sea. It is estimated that the Arctic Ocean has lost 40 percent of its sea ice

in the last few **decades.** And glaciers are retreating around the world, in the Alps, Tibet, Kenya, Antarctica, Peru, and Alaska.

Melting sea ice and glaciers also are causing our oceans to rise. Scientists predict that rising oceans will leave many coastal areas and places on land that are close to sea level underwater during this century.

Warming temperatures also are resulting in less snow and ice pack in the mountains during the winter. This in turn results in less fresh water (from snow melt) in streams, rivers, lakes, and underground **aquifers** during the rest of the year. This is leaving wildlife and human populations in some areas around the planet without enough water.

Melting glaciers deplete the snowpack.

Flooding

Too much rain can make it impossible for the ground to absorb water fast enough and can cause rivers to overflow. Flooding can damage or destroy wildlife habitat, houses, farms,

Flooding can damage cropland, resulting in food shortages.

and even towns and cities. Parts of Europe, North America, India, and Asia in the last few years have had the worst flooding in their recorded history. Mumbai, India, for example, had 37 inches of rain in one day in 2005, raising water levels in some places up to 7 feet and killing 1,000 people. Flooding can wash away soil from farms and spread diseases caused by bacteria that live in water. Flooding also can wash away coastal areas.

action: Flood Watch

Look at a globe or world map to find places that are most likely to be affected by rising oceans, such as coasts and islands. Identify places that are most likely to be affected by flooding, such as areas near large rivers and wetlands.

Students work in teams to create maps of local areas potentially threatened by flooding. They come up with plans for relocating housing and infrastructure to minimize flooding damage and danger.

http://www.ipcc.ch *Read the IPCC report.*

17

COOL fact

Soil is much more than "dirt." Soil is full of living things and nutrients that clean, recycle, and feed all life on Earth. Soil contains minerals, air, water, decomposed plants and animals, and living things, such as worms, centipedes, beetles, bacteria, and fungi. Without soil, the earth would be lifeless rock and sand.

Drought

Reduced springtime glacier melt or a lack of rain or snow dries land, lakes, streams, rivers, and underground water reserves. In many parts of the world drought is a serious problem that is expected to get much worse because of warming temperatures. One quarter of people (1.75 billion) worldwide do not have adequate drinking water, and this number will increase significantly in the coming decades.

Drought makes farming difficult or impossible because it makes soil infertile, or unable to support life. Dried up soil with few or no plants is more likely to **erode,** or be blown or washed away, because plants help hold soil together.

Drought also leads to fires, which can destroy forests and towns. Record-setting hot and dry conditions in 2004 in the forests around Fairbanks, Alaska, led to a fire that destroyed 6.3 million acres—an area about the size of New Hampshire.

Soil Layers

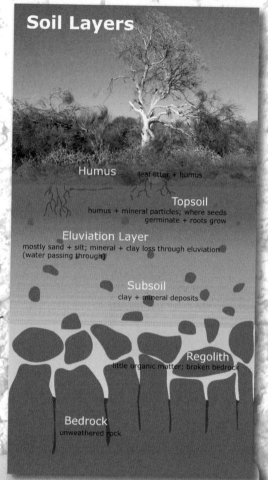

Humus — leaf litter + humus

Topsoil — humus + mineral particles; where seeds germinate + roots grow

Eluviation Layer — mostly sand + silt; mineral + clay loss through eluviation (water passing through)

Subsoil — clay + mineral deposits

Regolith — little organic matter; broken bedrock

Bedrock — unweathered rock

In healthy **fertile** soil, fresh organic matter from decaying leaves and plant roots in the humus and topsoil layers attracts worms and beetles. Worms and beetles create tunnels and leave openings called *pores.* This creates stable soil that is able to absorb and store more water, which supports plant life and helps keep the soil layers healthy.

During drought, plants die off, leaving less organic matter in the humus and topsoil. With nothing to hold it in place, the upper soil layers are more easily blown or washed away by wind and rain. Decreased organic matter in the soil supports fewer worms and beetles, making the soil hard and unable to absorb and hold water.

action: The Scoop on Soil

Learn more about the importance of soil in our world by playing the online game The Scoop on Soil at http://www .urbantext.uiuc.edu/soil/index.html.

Student pairs play the online game to learn about soil. Then the class works together to create a soil terrarium with organic matter, beetles, earthworms, centipedes, water, and sunlight.

Storm Chart

storms	damage	preparation

action: Storm Chart

What storms do you have where you live? Do online research on storms. Make a chart showing the common kinds of storms in your area, the kinds of damage they cause, and ways to prepare for and prevent such damage. For example, restoring natural flood zones for rivers helps reduce the impact of flooding by allowing wetlands and floodplains to absorb rainwater.

Student teams research different types of local storms. They discover records, frequency, damage, emergency responses, planning and preparation, political leader response, and so on. Then teams create charts illustrating their findings. Each team presents its chart with a brief summary to the class.

Storms

More and stronger storms most likely influenced by warming ocean waters have already happened around the world and are expected to worsen in our century. In 2004 a record-breaking 10 typhoons hit Japan, and four hurricanes hit Florida. In 2005 Hurricane Katrina destroyed much of the Gulf Coast, leaving thousands homeless and causing more than $100 billion in damage. In August of 2007 monsoons affected 20 million people in India, Nepal, and Bangladesh, killing hundreds and leaving many homeless. And just a few days later for the first time in recorded history a tornado hit Brooklyn, New York. In addition to causing destruction and homelessness, storms often lead to flooding and the spread of disease.

Disease

In many parts of the world cold temperatures help kill off microorganisms that cause diseases and insects that carry those diseases, such as ticks, lice, flies, and mosquitoes. Warmer temperatures are already making it possible for some diseases and their carriers to spread to new places. The spread of disease threatens people and animals all over the world, especially in places where there is poverty and people do not have medicine.

 http://www.who.int/en/ *Learn more about disease and epidemics.*

19

spinning gas and dust
4 billion years ago
rock formations

Life Is Changing

As weather conditions change, life on Earth is becoming very different very fast. The changes that have happened to Earth's climate in the last few decades and that are expected to continue usually happen very slowly over thousands or millions of years. By some estimates, our planet is now suddenly hotter than it has been in 650,000 years and is getting hotter all the time. It is difficult, perhaps impossible, for most life forms to adjust to such fast changes. This is because genetic adaptations in response to environmental changes occur slowly over generations. We have already learned how the sudden climate changes during the Younger Dryas Ice Age, for example, contributed to animal extinctions and human **population** losses.

Early Life

Earth has existed for 4.6 billion years, and life in simple forms started 3 billion years ago. The first living things were simple, tiny **microorganisms.** Some of these microorganisms were similar to bacteria and algae that live on Earth today. Then about 1 billion years ago more complex **multicellular** living things began appearing on Earth. Eventually these **organisms** evolved into plants and animals. In time an amazing assortment of plants and animals spread across the earth, in the oceans and on land: from jellyfish to juniper trees and goats to gadflies.

3 billion years ago

stromato

How Life Evolves

Through genetic changes over generations, animal and plant species become adapted to their environments. For example, some rabbits had stronger hind legs that worked well for running away from foxes and hawks. Those rabbits were less likely to

Earth Life Highlights

Stromatolites: Colonies of photosynthetic bacteria appear.
Eukaryotic cells: More complex cells appear.
Cambrian Explosion: Most of the major groups of animals appear quickly.
Permian-Triassic Extinction: Largest mass extinction in history of Earth occurs.
Tetrapods: First four-legged vertebrates appear on land.
Pelycosaurs: Intermediate stage between reptiles and mammals emerges.
Australopithecus: Early hominid closely related to humans appears.
Homo sapiens: The first modern humans emerge.

Paleozoic fish

Pelycos

be caught and eaten than rabbits who didn't have strong legs. So more rabbits with strong legs survived and had offspring, and most of their offspring had strong legs too. After many generations of passing along helpful genes, most rabbits had strong hind

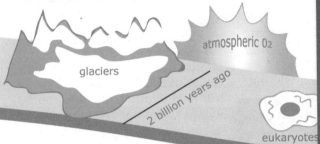

legs. This change, or adaptation, in response to environment is **evolution.**

All living things on Earth, including people, have evolved to be able to survive in their environment. Our adaptations enable most of us to find food, make shelters, avoid being hurt or killed, and have children.

action: Dino Time/ Human Time

Make a chart or graph to show the difference between how long dinosaurs lived (165 million years) and how long modern humans have lived (175,000 years). You might use a clock, bar graph, pie chart, or time line. Do some research to find out how long other kinds of animals have lived or once lived on Earth and add them to your chart or graph.

Students work in teams to research how long other kinds of life forms have lived on Earth and then make graphs to show the relative lengths of time. Students can learn about percentages using this activity and then represent the data in terms of percentages too.

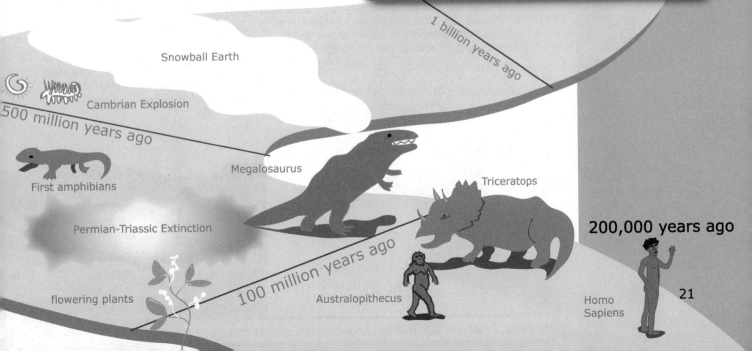

21

This Honolulu suburb is sprawling into the foothills. What kinds of animals can survive here?

HOT fact

The Baiji dolphin lived in the waters of the Yangtze River of eastern China for 20 million years until it became extinct in 2006. Overfishing, pollution, and busy shipping traffic in the river interfered with the Baiji's sonar method of finding food.

The Baiji dolphin, the Goddess of the Yangtze, is now extinct.

How Sudden Climate Change Affects Living Things

It takes many years, usually thousands or even millions, over many generations for living things to become adapted to their environments. For this reason, most species cannot survive in an environment experiencing sudden climate change. Some animals may find other places to live, and the seeds of some plants may spread to other places and survive, but most will not.

The mountain pine beetle has responded to climate change by taking only one year instead of two to regenerate. Now beetle populations are much larger and are killing many North American pine trees; the red trees shown here have died.

Most species cannot travel far from where they are born, and most of the ones that can are not able to find a place to live where their adaptations will allow them to survive.

This is especially true now because so much of the world has been taken over and changed by humans. Human cities, suburbs, villages, and farms have altered areas where animals and plant life once lived on Earth. Much plant and animal life still surviving today has already lost **habitat** and moved or spread to areas away from people. These life forms have smaller populations and fewer places left where they can survive. Have you noticed places where you live that have been destroyed to build houses, stores, or roads?

To create this gold mine in the Venezuelan rainforest, the land was logged and then flooded.

22

http://www.baiji.org *Learn more about the baiji.*

Endangered and Extinct Species

Because most living things cannot adapt to sudden climate change or move to new locations, many species have already died or become extinct. An **extinct species** no longer lives anywhere on Earth and never will exist again. Many species of butterfly, bird, toad, fish, salamander, bear, cat, monkey, lemur, dolphin, mushroom, flower, tree, shrub, and grass have gone extinct or are in danger of going extinct. Some people have estimated that another species goes extinct on Earth every 10 minutes!

What is one possible problem with removing an animal from the endangered species list?

action: Avoiding the Fate of the Dinosaurs

What advantages or skills do you think humans have that could help us avoid the fate of the dinosaurs? Make a list of your ideas and discuss them with a friend or family member.

Student teams of three or four discuss and list their ideas. Then they share their lists and talk together to make a class list of the best ideas.

action: Learn How to Help Endangered Species

There are over 1,300 different kinds of plants and animals on the U.S. Endangered Species List. These species have very low populations and are in danger of becoming extinct. Visit the Kid's Corner of the U.S. Fish and Wildlife Service Endangered Species Program to learn what you can do to help these species: http://www.fws.gov/endangered/kids/index.html.

In teams of two or three, students visit Kid's Corner and choose an action to help endangered species. Each team writes a short action plan and later reports about its progress to the class.

http://www.fws.ogov/endangered/kids/index.html *Help endangered species.*

Altered Ecosystems

Earth is made up of **ecosystems,** or interconnected groups of living things. These species share the same habitat and depend on one another for food, shelter, and reproduction.

Honeybees pollinate blueberries, apples, cherries, kiwis, avocados, pumpkins, watermelons, cucumbers, almonds, and many other things people eat.

For example, bees eat nectar and pollen from flowers. In return, flowers rely on bees to carry their pollen to other flowers for pollination, which allows them to reproduce, or make fruit with seeds to produce more flowers. In turn, animals, including people, eat the fruit of the plants that honey bees pollinate and help the plants by spreading their seeds.

COOL fact

About one-third of the food eaten by people comes from plants pollinated mostly by honeybees. Honeybees collect nectar from nearly 9 million flowers to make 1 pound of honey!

HOT fact

Honeybees are dying in huge numbers. People studying this "colony collapse disorder" have found that the bees' immune systems, which fight disease, are weakened, making it difficult for them to stay healthy. Pesticides, lost habitat, warming temperatures, and foreign viruses are possible causes.

Members of an ecosystem evolve together to survive in the same environment. When that environment changes suddenly, the relationships among species are disrupted and all members of the ecosystem are affected. For example, **coral reefs** support complex ecosystems in the ocean. An amazing variety of fish and other species such as shrimp, crab, sponges, turtles, snakes, worms, and starfish depend on coral reefs for food and shelter. But warming ocean waters are causing **coral** to die. When coral die, large numbers of plants and animals die too.

Healthy coral in the Seychelles and, at right, a partly bleached coral.

Mass Extinctions

When at least half of Earth's species become extinct in a relatively short amount of time, it is called a **mass extinction.** The earth has experienced five mass extinctions in its history, and currently it is going through its sixth.

The mass extinction that wiped out the dinosaurs 65 millions years ago is called the Cretaceous-Tertiary Extinction. It is probably the most well-known one, but it is only the second smallest. The Permian-Triassic Extinction, about 251 million years ago, was the largest in Earth's history. It is estimated that 90 to 95 percent of all species died off at that time. That means 90 to 95 of every 100 species became extinct! Most scientists believe that warming temperatures on Earth caused this period of mass extinction.

Most scientists agree that sudden climate change probably caused the extinction of

Mass Extinctions: The Big Six

mya = million years ago

1. Ordovician-Silurian
When: 465–440 mya
Why: global cooling, lowered sea levels
What: second biggest; at least 70% of all species

2. Devonian
When: 370–360 mya
Why: global cooling, lowered sea levels
What: up to 70% of all marine species

3. Permian-Triassic
When: 251–250 mya
Why: severe global warming, asteroid impact, or ongoing volcanic eruptons
What: largest mass extinction; maybe 90–95% of species

4. Triassic-Jurassic
When: 225–206 mya
Why: massive lava floods; global warming
What: many land vertebrates; 50% of marine animal species

5. Cretaceous-Tertiary
When: 65 mya
Why: asteroid impact or massive volcanic eruptions
What: 50% of all life; all nonavian dinosaurs

6. Cenozoic-Quarternary
When: 10,000 years ago–today
Why: habitat loss, overhunting, pollution, nonnative species introduction, and anthropogenic global warming
What: over 80 species per day

HOT fact

When coral reefs die it is called **coral bleaching** because they turn a dull whitish color (which is what bleach does to clothes in the laundry). Some scientists estimate that all ocean coral will die by the year 2050 if we don't act now to reduce climate change.

COOL fact

Scientists who study life in Earth's past are called *paleontologists.*

action: Signs of Spring

Think of all the wonderful signs of spring: trees blossoming, birds singing, bees humming, deer having fawns. Write a poem or paragraph describing what you love about spring. Think about sight, sound, touch, smell, and taste as you write. Now imagine what spring will be like on Earth if people do not stop climate change. Write another poem or paragraph of your thoughts.

Students illustrate their pieces and display the writings and illustrations on a class mural. They invite students from other classes to visit the mural and respond to it in writing on a Reactions Wall.

the dinosaurs too. Perhaps an asteroid slammed into Earth, or huge volcanic eruptions occurred, changing the world's climate. The mass extinction happening right now is unusual because it is being caused by a single species—humans.

There are always some species extinctions happening on Earth. The normal rate is one species dying off about every four years. Today, however, at least 30,000 species are going extinct each year. It is predicted that, unless we work immediately to reduce climate change, approximately 40 percent of species on the planet could be extinct in the next 40 years.

How Fast Is Climate Change Happening?

We know that climate change has already begun to affect weather patterns and ecosystems around the world. Increased drought, glacier melt, coral bleaching, and the extinction of species are some examples of the effects of our warming climate. Scientists believe that the effects of climate change will continue to increase during and after this century. Some changes will continue to take place in the next few years and decades, and others may take longer. How serious these changes will be depends on what people do right now to reduce the causes of climate change.

Chapter Summary

Climate change is causing Earth's weather to change. Some places are experiencing more flooding, melting sea ice and glaciers, drought, storms, and disease. Changes to Earth's environment are disrupting ecosystems and causing many species to become endangered or extinct. There have been five mass extinctions in Earth's history, and we are experiencing the sixth right now. The effects of climate change will continue to alter the earth during this century and the next. How quickly these changes happen depends on what people do right now.

The Causes of Climate Change: Our World out of Balance

> *If you have always done it that way,*
> *it is probably wrong.*
> —Charles Kettering

> *We have built a greenhouse, a human creation,*
> *where once there bloomed a sweet and wild garden.*
> —Bill McKibben

F or most of human history, people have lived in relative balance with other living things on Earth. Although some ancient peoples, such as the Clovis people 13,000 years ago, probably overhunted certain species in North America, there was enough land, fresh water, fresh air, and food on Earth for humans and most other species to coexist, or live together. Birds, mammals, fish, insects, reptiles, amphibians, trees, and other plant life thrived throughout the world. But in the last few hundred years the human population has exploded, and that balance has been lost.

The fact that there are so many people now living on our planet and using its resources is creating several kinds of imbalances. People are changing the balance of gases in our atmosphere, developing too much land, using up natural resources, and polluting our environment.

Too Much Greenhouse Gas in Our Atmosphere

Earth has a thin layer of gases, or **atmosphere,** that protects it from the cold temperatures of outer space. Earth's atmosphere is mostly made up of **nitrogen** (N_2) and oxygen (O_2).

There are other gases in our atmosphere in small, or trace,

COOL fact

Earth's gravitational pull keeps our atmosphere from drifting into space. Earth's atmosphere has five layers. The troposphere, where our weather occurs, is the closest layer. It is about 6 miles thick.

The blue band shows Earth's atmosphere. The depression in the cloud cover is Hurricane Emily.

The atmosphere on Mars is so thin it holds much less heat from the sun than Earth does. This makes Mars a very cold and probably lifeless place.

amounts. These trace gases include noble gases and **greenhouse gases.** Earth's greenhouse gases are carbon dioxide, methane, nitrous oxide, water vapor, and ozone. These greenhouse gases hold in some of the sun's heat, making it warm enough here for life to thrive. Without greenhouse gases in our atmosphere, too much of the sun's heat would bounce back out into space, and Earth would be very cold, like Mars.

When there is too much greenhouse gas in our atmosphere, it traps too much of the sun's heat and causes the earth to warm up. That is what is causing climate change today. You might say it is too much of a good thing.

Some solar radiation escapes back into space. Some is reflected back again to Earth off the greenhouse gases in the atmosphere. When more heat is trapped, and less heat escapes, global warming occurs.

Earth's Atmospheric Gases

N_2 78%

O_2 21%

noble gases + greenhouse gases 1%

The noble gases in our atmosphere include argon, neon, helium, krypton, and xenon.

solar radiation

atmosphere

action: Greenhouse Effect

You can observe the greenhouse effect with a simple experiment. Place a piece of clear glass over the open top of a box. The piece of glass is like our atmosphere. Place the covered box in the sun for 30 minutes. Then use a thermometer to measure the temperature inside the box and compare it to the temperature outside the box. How do they compare?

Students work in pairs to conduct the experiment, using glass in different thicknesses. They create charts to show their results. As a class, they discuss the real-world implications of increased greenhouse gases.

Carbon Dioxide

Carbon monoxide, or CO, is what we think of as pollution. It is the smelly, black smoke that comes from burning engines, fires, and factories. **Carbon dioxide,** or CO_2, also comes from engines, fires, and factories, but it is invisible, has no smell, and is not harmful to breathe.

Carbon dioxide is the main greenhouse gas currently causing climate change. Although Earth's atmosphere has very little carbon dioxide compared to other gases, even a small change to the amount of carbon dioxide greenhouse gas can cause enormous changes to Earth's climate.

Carbon dioxide mainly comes from burning **fossil fuels**: oil, coal, and natural gas. We burn fossil fuels to make the electricity we use to light, heat, and cool our homes, buildings, and factories and to run our appliances and machines. We burn oil to run engines in cars, trucks, farm equipment, airplanes, and lawn mowers. Carbon dioxide also comes from fires. About 30 percent of carbon dioxide **emissions** each year results from cooking fires and from burning forests and brush. In places like the Amazon Rainforest, people burn large areas to create land for farming and raising cattle.

Scientists can measure how much carbon dioxide is in Earth's atmosphere and compare the amounts at different times in Earth's history. They predict that if we continue releasing carbon dioxide at the rate we have been in the last 50 years, it will be about double (500 parts per million) what it was before the Industrial Revolution about 200 years ago. This could raise the world's average temperature by about 5 to 8 degrees Fahrenheit by 2050. This increase in global temperature may not sound like a lot, but it has huge consequences for ecosystems everywhere.

The oceans take in about one-third, or 25 million tons, of the carbon dioxide released into Earth's atmosphere every day. This is making seawater more

action: Carbon Monoxide Versus Carbon Dioxide

Draw a picture of where carbon monoxide and carbon dioxide come from and the different ways they harm our environment. You can use words in your picture to help explain.

Students display their pictures in a hallway exhibit to help educate the rest of the school about carbon dioxide and carbon monoxide.

acidic, which is killing sea life such as coral and shellfish and causing algal blooms. Algal blooms are an overgrowth of algae at the surface of the water. The algae in some algal blooms release poisons that harm sea life and the animals (including humans) that feed on such sea life. Algal blooms can also harm ocean ecosystems by preventing oxygen from entering ocean water.

Too Much Fossil Fuel

People haven't been trying to change the climate on Earth. Climate change is something that is happening because of the way people are living and because there are now so many of us on Earth. Countries around the world are using huge amounts of fossil fuel to make energy. This pumps carbon dioxide into Earth's atmosphere, causing climate change. Here are some examples of things people do that pump millions of tons of carbon dioxide into Earth's atmosphere every single day:

- People use electricity to heat and cool homes and buildings and to run appliances and machines. Power companies burn coal, oil, and natural gas to make that electricity.

The increased amounts of CO$_2$ entering our oceans are killing **aquatic** *life.*

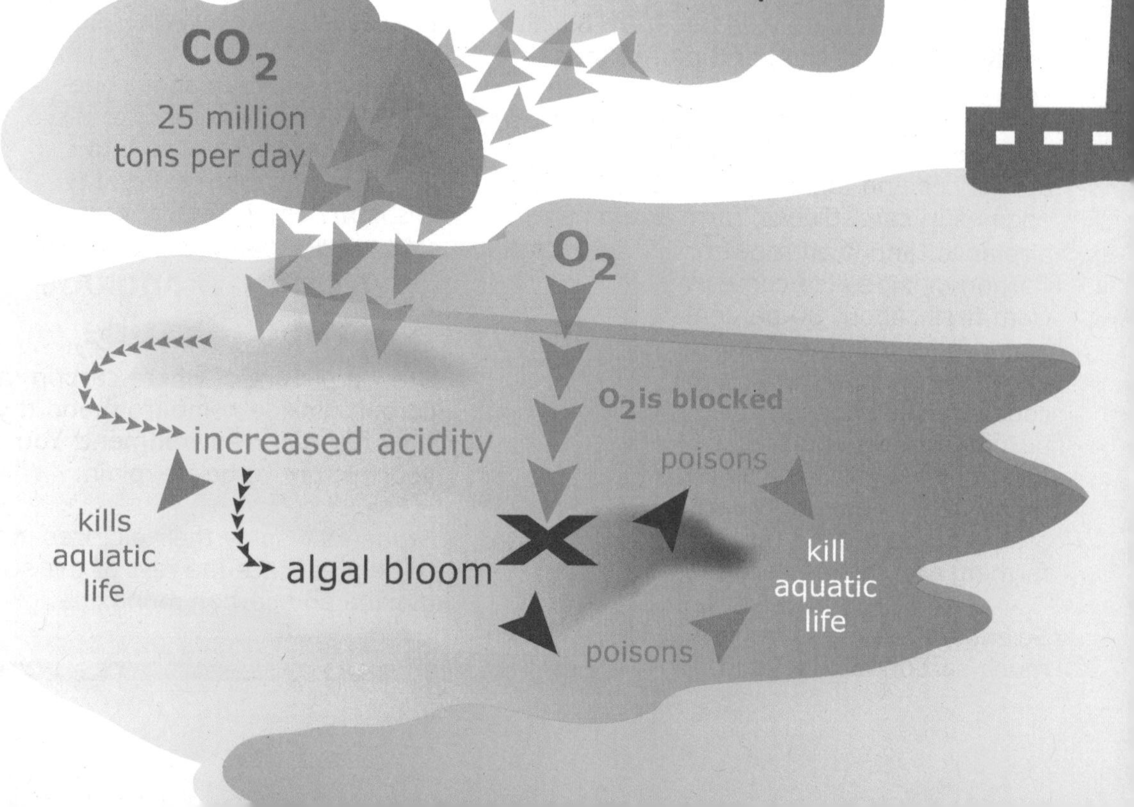

CO$_2$
25 million tons per day

O$_2$

O$_2$ is blocked

increased acidity

poisons

kills aquatic life

algal bloom

poisons

kill aquatic life

HOT fact

Measurements of carbon dioxide emissions in 2007 showed that China is now releasing more CO_2 than the United States is, making China the biggest emitter in the world.

Pollution in Shanghai, China.

- People buy billions of products, and manufacturing companies use electricity to make and package those products.
- People drive oil-burning cars to get around.
- Large farms use oil-burning machines and trucks to plant, harvest, and ship food around the world.
- Shipping companies use oil-burning trucks, ships, and airplanes to send products around the world.
- People eat more meat than they need. Raising and transporting cattle and other animals uses much more energy from fossil fuels than growing fruits, vegetables, and grains does.
- Human overpopulation is creating even more demand for electricity and other forms of energy.

Too Many People

The **overpopulation** of people on Earth is one of the biggest problems in the world today. In many ways it is the root of climate change and many of the major problems we all now face on our planet.

There are now about 6.5 billion people on Earth and a lot more on the way in the coming decades. That means there are now far more of us than the earth is years old (4.6 billion years).

With so many of us suddenly living on Earth and using its natural resources—land, water, air, trees, food, fossil fuels—we are crowding out other life forms

31

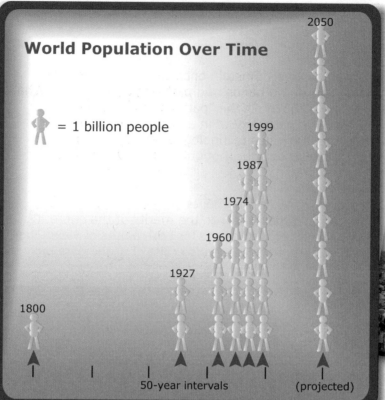

World Population Over Time

= 1 billion people

2050

1999

1987

1974

1960

1927

1800

50-year intervals

(projected)

Can you think of reasons why the world's human population has grown so quickly in recent decades?

On a hot day, the beach fills up with people. What other species could live here?

and releasing enormous amounts of carbon dioxide into our atmosphere.

Too Much Electricity Use

Modern humans have been living on the earth for about 175,000 years. Until only about a hundred years ago people lived without electricity. The human species survived for

thousands of years without electricity, appliances, power tools, televisions, and computers. Yet now many of us feel so dependent on electricity we use it all day long every single day.

We leave on lights, heaters, televisions, radios, and computers in rooms we're not in. We heat or cool our homes while we're gone at school or work all day. We use machines and appliances such as electric can openers and toothbrushes to do things we could do by hand.

What do all these wires say about our reliance on electricity? Imagine what our skies would look like without eletcrical wires and telephone poles.

http://www.opr.princeton.edu/popclock/ *Watch world population increase.*

action: Tune in and Turn off

Take an Energy Tour of your home. How many things use electricity? Make a list of all the things. Then circle the things you could use less or do without. Share your list with your family members. Ask them for ideas about how to reduce the amount of electricity your household uses. Then post your ideas where everyone can refer to them.

Students take an Energy Tour of their classroom and/or school. They invite other classes to do the same thing and present their ideas to the school administration. (Students must understand that some ideas may not be practical because of school policy, lack of funds, or state or federal law.)

HOT fact

To store all our stuff, many of us buy bigger and bigger houses. The average house in America today is twice as big as the average house was in 1970.

What does this store clothing display seem to say about resources? What is the reality?

Too Much Stuff

People in the United States have three times as many possessions today as they had 50 years ago and far more than at any other time in human history. Many of us have more clothes, toys, furniture, appliances, and cars than we need or even use. We are overstuffed with stuff!

As we buy more and more things, manufacturing companies use more and more energy to make and transport those things around the world. Just about everything we buy results in more carbon dioxide being released into our atmosphere. Making "stuff" also uses important natural

action: Animal Simplicity

Have you ever thought about the fact that animals don't buy or own things? Just about the only "stuff " they need is food and a safe, warm place to sleep and have babies. Animals have feathers, fur coats, and blubber to keep them warm and sharp senses to help them find food. At one time people lived more like other animals. Imagine life without most of your stuff. How would it be more difficult? How would it be better? Write a journal entry of a day in your new simpler life.

Students share their entries. Together they come up with a list of ways to simplify their lives.

resources and creates vast amounts of pollution. And studies show that as long as we have the basics of what we need, people are actually happier with less.

Too Much Driving

As with electricity, for thousands of years people lived without motorized transportation. There were no cars or trains or buses or trucks or airplanes. Yet today many people use their cars to go everywhere and can't imagine life without them. People spend hours each day commuting in cars to work and school.

Many people feel they have no choice but to drive to the places they need to be. There was a time when people worked at home and grew their own food or

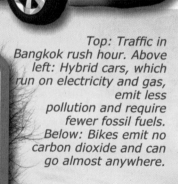

Top: Traffic in Bangkok rush hour. Above left: Hybrid cars, which run on electricity and gas, emit less pollution and require fewer fossil fuels. Below: Bikes emit no carbon dioxide and can go almost anywhere.

action: Park It

Take a Family Driving Survey. Talk with all the members of your family who drive and ask them to help you figure out the reasons you all drive. Also estimate how much time your family spends driving. Then work together to come up with a list of ideas for how to cut back on the amount of driving your family does. Can you combine errands, take public transportation, car pool (ride with a group), ride bikes, or walk? Post your *Park It* ideas where everyone in your family can see them.

Students work together to start a bike-to-school or carpool program.

http://www.youtube.com/watch?v=qk6YxhKH590 *Get inspired to bike.*

lived in communities where they could walk to school and the marketplace. Now in many parts of the world towns and cities are set up so that people have to drive.

Industrial Farms

At one time people grew much of their own food on small family farms. They raised a few animals, and the manure from those animals helped fertilize their crops. They lived in relative balance with nature. Now much of the food in the United States and other parts of the world is grown on very large industrial farms that are not in balance with nature.

These farms use chemical pesticides to kill crop-eating insects and fertilizers to make their crops grow fast and big. Such **agricultural chemicals** pollute the air and water and harm the soil, leading to erosion.

Industrial farms use big machines to plant, maintain, and harvest their crops. These

Producing 2 pounds of beef releases 72 pounds of carbon dioxide.

machines produce large amounts of carbon dioxide. Such farms release additional carbon dioxide when they transport their crops to grocery stores and markets around the world.

Too Much Meat

Raising animals for meat takes far more energy than growing other kinds of food like vegetables, grains, and fruit. Much of the world's rainforests have been destroyed to create cattle rangeland to provide meat for people to eat. Rainforests help cool the earth by absorbing carbon dioxide. When they are cut and burned, this important function is lost and carbon dioxide is released from fires.

The large feedlots and buildings where many animals are now raised for meat give off methane, which is a greenhouse gas. Like carbon dioxide, methane builds up in our atmosphere and contributes to global warming by trapping heat from the sun.

Cropdusting: A biplane drops chemical pesticides on a farm. Crops such as cotton may receive as many as 10 chemical dustings in a growing season. Agricultural chemicals cause birth defects, cancer, immune diseases, and death in local wildlife and human communities.

35

Rainforest Deforestation

Tropical rainforests are an extremely important part of Earth's global ecosystem. Although they now cover less than 5 percent of the earth's surface, they produce 40 percent of Earth's oxygen and contain more than half of the world's species.

Many medicines of the world come from plants in tropical rainforests. Tropical rainforests also do important things for Earth's climate. They regulate rainfall and absorb huge amounts of carbon dioxide.

During the 20th century, enormous areas of tropical rainforests were destroyed, or deforested. This **deforestation** continues today, with large areas being cut down or burned and hundreds of species going extinct each day. The main reasons for this deforestation are logging for lumber and clearing areas for farming and grazing cattle. In places with poor economies, often people have no choice but to destroy natural resources to make

Top: The Borneo rainforest. Bottom: A jungle in Lacandon, Mexico, was burned by local people to make room for farming.

money to survive. This can be helpful for a while, but it is not a **sustainable,** or long-term, solution.

Many of the people who live in the forests are losing their homes and way of life. And the fires in the rainforests are releasing more carbon dioxide into our atmosphere. Losing these vital areas of Earth's ecosystem is very dangerous for our climate and for all living things.

action: Locating the World's Tropical Rainforests

Tropical rainforests only grow in a narrow area of Earth between the latitudes 22.5° North and 22.5° South of the equator, between the Tropic of Capricorn and the Tropic of Cancer. Find these latitudes on a globe or world map and locate the continents where tropical rainforests grow: Central and South America, Africa, Asia, and Australia.

Students find Earth's tropical areas on a map. Then they work in teams to draw the continents and color in the rainforest areas. Students could also create different maps showing the amount of rainforest 20 years ago versus today.

Pablo Fajardo (1972–) is the main prosecuting lawyer in one of the biggest environmental lawsuits in history. Fajardo grew up in an extremely poor family in Ecuador. He began working in the fields as a child, helped take care of his 12 siblings, and earned his law degree through a correspondence course. For his first case, he was hired to fight a large oil company, one of the biggest, most powerful corporations in the world.

Fajardo represents 30,000 people who live in the Amazon Rainforest in Ecuador, where the company

Pablo Fajardo

drilled oil for 30 years. Fajardo argues that during the drilling the company dumped over 18 billion gallons of **toxic** waste into Amazon rivers and streams that local people and wildlife depend on for drinking and bathing.

Suffering with high cancer rates and other health problems, the people decided to sue the company to clean up the mess, which was reportedly 30 times larger than the Exxon Valdez oil spill. If Fajardo wins, the company may have to pay six billion dollars. To learn more about the case, visit http://www.amazonwatch.org.

action: Learn How to Help Preserve Tropical Rainforests

Visit http://www.kids.mongabay.com/elementary/601.html to learn more about tropical rainforests and what you can do to help save them from further deforestation.

Teams of two or three students visit the site to find specific ways to help the rainforest. Each team chooses a topic and creates a poster illustrating one way to help. Students might host a rainforest day for the rest of the school, featuring the posters, maps showing the disappearing rainforest, images of the diverse species found there, and food from the cultures that live there.

37

http://www.amazonwatch.org *Follow Fajardo's case.*

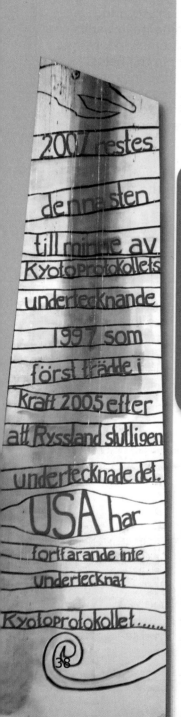

Laws That Don't Protect the Environment

The governments of many countries around the world are not doing enough to protect the environment and reduce climate change. Many nations do not have strong enough laws to prevent people from burning fossil fuels, harming wildlife, and homes. Some laws also make it easier for very large farms than small farms to survive.

The Kyoto Treaty

Leaders from around the world created guidelines called the Kyoto Treaty for all countries to follow to help reduce climate

action: U.S. Mayors' Climate Protection Agreement

Find out if your city has joined the U.S. Mayors' Climate Protection Agreement: http://www.seattle.gov/mayor/climate. If it has, visit your city government website or contact its office to find out what people in your community are doing to reduce climate change. If your city hasn't joined the Agreement, write or call your mayor and city council to ask them to join.

Teams of students research what your city's mayor is doing about climate change. They share their findings with the class. If your city has not joined the agreement, students can write letters to send to your mayor to ask him or her to join.

polluting. Many places also do not have laws that require people to reduce energy use in their homes and businesses.

Some laws actually help support the practices of large oil, coal, and natural gas companies that sell harmful fossil fuels, as well as companies that make toxic chemicals used in farming, manufacturing,

Left: This stone in Stadsparken, Sweden, was erected in 2007 in memory of the Kyoto Treaty (which Sweden signed in 1997). The words on the stone explain that the United States still has not signed the agreement.

change. The Kyoto Treaty says that all countries have to promise to reduce how much carbon dioxide they are producing.

Every major country in the world signed the agreement except for the United States and Australia. Many people around the world were very disappointed that the United States did not sign the agreement, especially since it is the second biggest producer of carbon dioxide in the world.

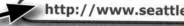 http://www.seattle.gov/mayor/climate *Has your city joined?*

A group of mayors from cities around the United States created the U.S. Mayors' Climate Protection Agreement. These mayors decided to follow the Kyoto Treaty guidelines in their own cities. From Seattle, Washington, to Chicago, Illinois, to Charleston, South Carolina, they promised to "meet or beat" the Kyoto guidelines.

Climate Change Isn't the Only Problem

We've talked about how climate change is caused by an imbalance in our atmosphere. Large amounts of carbon dioxide are building up, trapping too much sunlight and heating up our world. But there are other problems that are seriously harming our home planet. These problems are worsening the effects of climate change because they are damaging the earth and making life harder for living things everywhere.

Overdevelopment

People around the world are using more and more land for housing and commercial developments, large industrial farms, and cattle grassland. Vast wildlife areas have been taken over by people. Natural habitats like forests, wetlands, deserts, and prairies have been destroyed, driving away or killing the animals and plants who lived there. Especially in towns and cities, there are fewer and fewer wild, undeveloped places for nonhuman species.

Pollution

We pollute our land, air, oceans, rivers, lakes, and aquifers (fresh water underground) with smoke, chemicals, sewage, and garbage.

HOT fact

Over 6,000 acres of land are developed in the United States every day.

A housing development in California. Notice the cleared hill in the background awaiting more houses.

A forest in Japan cleared for a major development.

Concrete housing, which can be built rapidly, in the final stages of construction.

39

Garbage piled on a street.

HOT fact

Thousands of sea turtles die each year from eating plastic bags in the ocean, which they mistake for jellyfish. The bags get caught in their intestines and cause them to starve to death.

Pollution sickens and kills plants, insects, fish, shellfish, amphibians, reptiles, birds, and mammals

(including people!) every day all around the world.

Smoke from factories, power plants, and automobiles causes acid rain and smog. Chemical pollutants from farms, manufacturing companies, and home cleaning products cause birth defects and diseases like cancer. Human and animal

HOT fact

Bluefin Tuna, Chilean Sea Bass, and Atlantic Halibut are examples of fish species whose populations are threatened from overfishing.

40

Eco-Hero

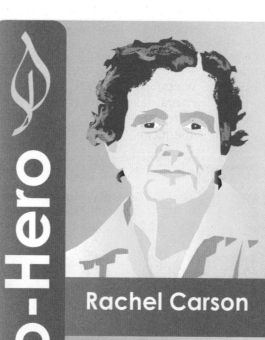

Rachel Carson

The ecologist and writer **Rachel Carson** (1907–1964) grew up in a simple farmhouse in rural Pennsylvania, where she learned from her mother to love nature. Her best-selling book *Silent Spring* was published in 1962. In it she warned about the harmful effects of using pesticides in farming.

She also appeared before the U.S. Congress to explain the dangers of chemical pollution.

Chemical companies tried to discredit her, but her writings and actions helped educate people and start a powerful environmental movement to help the earth. This movement continues today with people like you working to fight climate change!

action: Lose the Plastic!

List all the things in your life made of plastic. Then think of ways you and your family can reduce your use of these items. For example, bring cloth bags for shopping, use reusable metal water bottles instead of plastic ones, and avoid products with plastic packaging.

Teams of students research the problems of plastic garbage and toxic chemicals released from plastic products in our environment. Then they hold a Lose the Plastic Education Day in which they exhibit informational posters about the problems with plastic and their ideas for reducing people's use of it at home, in school, and in the community.

sewage from cities, farms, and fish farms spreads harmful bacteria that lead to diseases like cholera and avian flu. Garbage from urban areas collects in landfills and oceans, releasing more chemicals and harming animals who eat it.

Poverty often creates homelessness. A homeless man sleeps on a street in New York.

Poverty

Among the people of the world, there are also serious imbalances. While some people have more than they need, millions do not have the basics that they need to live a healthy life. **People who live in poverty may not have a safe and clean place to live, enough food, fresh drinking water, medicine, sewage disposal, or access to education. About half the people in the world live on less than two dollars a day. About 30,000 children die each day from poverty. Over half the children in the world receive no education.**

Although poor people in general produce fewer carbon emissions because they often do not have

Toxic runoff from metallic sulfide mining in Ontario, Canada.

electricity or cars, they are the ones who will suffer the most from climate change. This is because they have fewer resources to deal with problems such as drought, storms, flooding, and disease. Because poor people must do whatever they can to survive, they often cannot make choices that are healthy for the environment. We have already talked about how people in the Amazon Rainforest are cutting down the forest to raise cattle so that they can make money selling beef.

Overuse of Natural Resources

Natural resources are things from the earth that people use. They include water, soil, forests, plants, fish, iron ore (metals), and rock. When people overuse natural resources, they harm ecosystems and take more than the earth can restore naturally.

People are drying up rivers, lakes, and aquifers by building dams, taking too much water to irrigate crops, and not allowing these water sources to restore themselves. We are cutting down forested areas without replanting and allowing time for trees to regrow. We are catching fish and not giving them a chance to reproduce and replenish their populations. And we are taking over too much land and not leaving enough for wildlife.

In many parts of the world, water is scarce, forests are gone, very

Circular crop irrigation in Madagsacar. All the land around the irrigated circles is parched.

few fish are left, and wildlife habitat is destroyed. There are not enough natural resources to support the animals and people who live there. One-third of the world's population is experiencing a shortage of water. Forty countries face food shortages so severe that their people must rely on help from other countries.

Chapter Summary

Climate change is the result of imbalances in our world. There is too much carbon dioxide in our atmosphere trapping too much heat from the sun, and there are too many people on Earth using too many resources and creating too much waste. Carbon dioxide comes from people burning fossil fuels and forests. People burn fossil fuels for electricity, transportation, manufacturing, and industrial farming. They burn tropical rainforests to clear land for farming and raising cattle. Other problems on Earth are making climate change worse: laws that don't protect the environment, overdevelopment, pollution, poverty, and overuse of natural resources.

How People Can Stop Climate Change

COOL fact

Wind turbines create energy on large wind farms and also can be installed in individual homes. Find out more at the American Wind Energy Association website: http://www.awea.org/smallwind/.

Climate change is a serious and complicated problem. There are many things that people are doing that are harming the earth and living things. But there are also many things people can do to heal the earth and help living things. Societies around the world are starting to make bold changes to reduce the causes and effects of climate change. People need to continue to work hard to make changes in governments, nations, cities, towns, businesses, schools, and homes. Here are some ways communities around the world can make things better for our global environment.

Use Renewable Energy

One of the best ways to reduce climate change is to use **renewable energy** instead of fossil fuel energy. Renewable energy won't run out and doesn't harm the environment. Fossil fuel energy from oil, coal, and natural

Wind turbines in the Baltic Sea near Samsø, Denmark.

A solar panel collects energy from the sun and converts it into electricity or heat.

gas is not renewable because it will run out and obtaining it and using it hurt the planet.

There are many kinds of renewable energy that people are using already. **Solar energy** comes from sunlight, **wind power** comes from the wind, and **hydropower** comes from moving water. These alternative sources of energy can be used to make electricity.

An electric car parked at a public recharging station.

Why Do People Still Use Fossil Fuels?

It seems obvious that people should start using renewable sources of energy and stop using harmful coal, oil, and natural gas. So why haven't we? There are three main reasons.

Society Is Still Set Up to Use Fossil Fuels. Our systems for making electricity and delivering it to people are set up to use fossil fuels. Most of the engines that run our cars, trucks, planes, ships, and so on are built to use oil. It takes time and money to change to renewable energy sources. New energy plants need to be built to make electricity from renewable sources like the sun and wind. More cars that run on alternative power need to be built so we stop burning oil. These changes are already happening, but we need to work harder to make them happen faster.

Governments can help by creating **incentives** for people to switch to renewable energy. Incentives are laws that encourage people to do something. Often individuals and businesses need

 http://www.environmentaldefense.org/page.cfm?tagID=820 *Take action against CO_2.*

At the National Renewable Energies Laboratory, visitors inspect peel-and-stick panels that can turn sun rays into energy. The visit was part of the Udall Legacy Bus Tour, a cross-country bus trip for graduates of the Morris K. Udall environmental education program. The bus ran on biodiesel fuel (made from corn) and was **carbon neutral.**

incentives to help motivate them to change their habits.

People Are Still Learning How to Use Renewable Energy Sources.

We are still unsure about the best ways to use renewable energy sources. People who know a lot about these alternative energies need to work with others in electricity companies and car companies to decide how to use them. If these people work together they can start making changes to reduce the use of fossil fuel energy and help prevent further climate change.

Most Laws Still Don't Support the Use of Renewable Energy.

Many of our laws still help support large companies that sell oil, coal, and natural gas. These laws make it difficult for smaller companies who want to offer renewable energy to get started. Our government is meant to protect its citizens and our environment, but sometimes it protects big companies instead.

You can help change this by writing to your state and federal congresspeople to tell them you want them to reduce climate change. Find out which politicians support the environment and ask your parents to vote for them. You can also volunteer at political and environmental organizations that are working to fight climate change. Some day you may even decide to run for office to help the environment.

Vote Green

"Vote green" can mean vote for someone in the Green Party. But it also can mean voting for officials who will work to protect our environment.

action: Sign up for Green Energy

Many power companies allow their customers to buy their power from renewable energy instead of fossil fuel sources like coal plants. Have your parents contact your local power company to sign up to receive your power from renewable sources.

If your local energy company offers green energy options, students compose letters to take home to their parents explaining why they should consider switching to green energy from their local power company.

The average American meal includes food from five different countries.

Change the Way We Live

Climate change is starting to affect people everywhere and will continue to affect us all more and more. To make a real difference, we all have to get involved to make changes in our homes, schools, neighborhoods, businesses, cities, states, and nations. Each of us needs to think about what we can do to help. Here are some ways we can change our lifestyles to reduce climate change.

Build Better Public Transportation

Communities can provide better and more extensive public transportation systems so people drive less. Public transportation reduces gasoline consumption, car manufacturing, traffic congestion, and pollution.

Use Less Plastic

Huge amounts of oil and other chemicals are used to make plastic, adding to climate change and polluting our world.

Buying preowned items at garage sales or through freecycle websites keeps those items from being thrown into landfills and reduces the need to make new products.

Businesses can change this by not making products with plastic, and individuals can help by not buying plastic products or by using recycled plastic instead.

Plastic bottles recycled as lights.

Buy Less Stuff

We can buy fewer things. Many of us, especially in the United States, have far more than we need or even actually use. We live in homes bigger than we

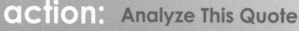

action: Analyze This Quote

The Greek philosopher Epictetus said, "It is impossible for a man to learn what he thinks he already knows." Try rewriting this quote in your own words. How does it apply to climate change? What can you learn from it? Share your thoughts with a family member or friend. Ask them what they think the quote means.

Students work in pairs to discuss their thoughts about the quote. Each pair creates a sentence restating the quote. Pairs share their sentences with the class. Together students discuss how they think the quote relates to climate change.

need, with rooms that sit empty much of the time. Until very recently, human beings lived well with much less, and we can learn to again.

Buy Locally Grown Food

It takes 17 times less oil to transport and refrigerate food locally than nonlocally. Locally grown food is fresher and therefore healthier and tastier to eat. Buying locally grown food is also good for your community because it provides local jobs and keeps farmland from being developed.

Buy Locally Made Products

Like buying locally grown food, buying locally made products saves energy for shipping and supports your own community.

You can find locally grown food at the nearest farmers' market. This one is in Madison, Wisconsin.

Buy Organic and Renewable Clothing

If all cotton farmers started growing their crops organically, or without harmful chemicals, world pollution would be dramatically reduced. Buying clothing, blankets, towels, and other products made from organic cotton or from renewable materials such as hemp and bamboo helps the environment and reduces people's exposure to chemicals on their skin.

Buy Organic Food

Organic farming uses 30 percent less energy to produce the same amount of food and does not pollute the land, water, and air. Buying organic food encourages farmers to stop using chemicals and encourages our government to support organic farming.

Use Recycled Products

We can support the **conservation** of natural resources by using products, such as paper, furniture, flooring, and shoes, made from recycled materials.

Global pesticide use

conventional cotton farming 25%

Handbags made from recycled paper.

Buy Sustainably Grown Wood

We can buy lumber and wood products like furniture grown in sustainably managed forests. These are forests where people only remove some of the trees and replant so that the forest continues to grow. Buying sustainably grown wood helps protect Earth's remaining forests from being chopped down for lumber. Look for the Smartwood certification stamp when you buy wood products. Or buy fast-growing wood such as bamboo.

Buy Used Homes

We can help protect more wilderness from being destroyed to build new homes by buying existing homes in older neighborhoods. Buying a home that has already been built also saves energy, trees, and other natural resources.

Compost

Composting is nature's recycling program. It is simply allowing your food cuttings and leftovers to decay naturally. With help from rainwater and sunlight, over time bacteria and small animals like worms, beetles, and slugs help break down composted food into rich soil. This soil then can be used to fertilize a lawn or garden.

This building scaffolding (wrapped in green) in Hong Kong is made entirely of bamboo. Bamboo is a fast-growing sustainable wood.

Use Renewable Energy

Power companies, automobile companies, and other manufacturing companies that make products like clothing,

Compost bins made from pallets.

furniture, electronics, and toys can switch to renewable sources of energy to run their plants. Homeowners and landlords can install solar panels to provide

48

A biodiesel pump to fuel cars.

power in homes and buildings. Towns and cities can invest money in renewable energy sources for their communities.

Drive Energy-Efficient Cars

We can choose cars that use less or no gasoline. There are now cars that run on alternate sources of energy, such as biodiesel made from vegetable oil and hydrogen.

A mural in Chicago.

Drive Less

We can use public transportation, carpool, work from home, walk or ride a bike, and combine errands.

Eat Less Meat

Eating less or no meat reduces energy consumption, methane gas, and the

potential for disease outbreak. It also can help reduce the number of animals forced to live in unnatural, often horrible living conditions. And it can reduce deforestation, often done to make rangeland for cattle.

Have Fewer Children

People can help reduce human overpopulation by having fewer children. Many people believe that it is best for the earth for families to have no more than one child.

Make Homes Energy Efficient

Homes can be made more energy efficient by installing better insulation, low-flow toilets and showers, cisterns for water

In the 2006 Solar Decathlon, 18 international college teams competed to build the most energy-efficient solar-powered home. The homes had to generate enough energy also to run an electric car. Here are the teams and, behind them on the Washington, D.C., Mall, their entries.

 http://www.solardecathlon.org *See the decathlon entries.*

Environmentalist and peace activist **Wangari Maathai** (1940–) started the Green Belt Movement in Kenya in 1977. Her goal was to help women and improve the environment in Africa, which had suffered from widespread deforestation. Over the last 30 years, the movement's women volunteers have planted 40 million trees. Their current goal is to plant

Wangari Maathai

one billion trees across the world! In 2004 Maathai became the first African woman to win the Nobel Peace Prize. Today she serves in the Kenyan Parliament as the Minister of Environment, Natural Resources, and Wildlife.

recycling, and renewable energy sources like solar panels.

Plant Trees

Trees and plants provide oxygen and absorb carbon dioxide. We can help reduce carbon dioxide, improve our air, provide habitat for wildlife, prevent soil erosion, and create shade and beauty by planting and growing **native species** of trees and plants.

Recycle

We can **recycle** instead of throwing things into the trash, which then gets buried in landfills or incinerated. Many communities have systems for recycling glass, metal, plastic, cardboard, and paper waste, so a great deal of garbage can actually be recycled into something useful again.

Reuse Stuff

We can pass along and donate used clothes, toys, cars, and more instead of throwing them away. We also can buy used items instead of new ones. This reduces the need to use energy and natural resources to make things and decreases the amount of waste in landfills and oceans.

 http://www.greenbeltmovement.org *Join the Green Belt.*

Switch to Fluorescent Lightbulbs

Switching to fluorescent lightbulbs is a great way to reduce electricity usage. Fluorescent lightbulbs use one quarter the energy of conventional incandescent lightbulbs and last about 10 times longer.

Unplug Appliances and Electronics

We can reduce the enormous energy drain from appliances and electronics equipment by unplugging them when they are not on. Plugging things into power strips that can be turned on and off easily with a switch is a convenient way to stop the energy drain without having to routinely plug and unplug electrical cords.

Vote for Politicians Who Support the Environment

We can vote for and support politicians who will pass laws to reduce climate change and protect our environment from pollution and development.

Chapter Summary

There are many things people can do to reduce climate change. We can use renewable energy, improve public transportation, drive less, drive energy-efficient cars, vote for environmentalist politicians, plant trees, make homes more energy efficient, recycle and reuse, buy less, buy sustainably grown wood, have fewer children, buy organic food and clothing, buy locally produced food and products, eat less or no meat, unplug appliances when not in use, and switch to fluorescent lightbulbs.

action: Unplug the Energy Hogs!

About 40 percent of home energy use is for appliances and electronics that aren't even turned on! These hogs constantly drain energy from electrical outlets even when they are turned off. Take a survey of the appliances in your home. How many are plugged in all the time? Talk with your family about keeping them unplugged when not in use. Work together to plug them into power strips that you can easily switch on and off.

Students take a similar survey of the classroom and make a plan to keep the hogs unplugged.

action: Be an Energy Hog Buster!

Play a fun Energy Hog Busting game online at http://www.energyhog.org.

Students use the Green Schools Tool Kit to study energy consumption at the school. The Tool Kit is available from http://www.ase.org/section/program/greenschl/gsresources. They also do activities found at http://www.energyhog.org/adult/educators.htm.

5 | What People Are Already Doing to Fight Climate Change

Never doubt that a small group of thoughtful, committed citizens can change the world. Indeed, it is the only thing that ever has.
—Margaret Mead

People of all ages all over the world are working hard to fight climate change and related problems. Whatever their age, country, gender, or background, what they have in common is the fact that they care. Some of them started out with great ideas about how to make things better. Others started out not really knowing what to do and figured it out along the way.

In this chapter, you'll read two Case Studies about some people who are taking bold steps to help the earth and support living things. You'll also find out about many other organizations that, in their different ways, are confronting climate change and working to lessen its effects.

Case Study 1

Ashton Hayes Goes Carbon Neutral

In 2005 residents of the small town of Ashton Hayes decided to make their village the first in England to stop releasing carbon dioxide into the atmosphere. "We want our children and future generations to know that we tried to do our bit to stem global warming and also encourage other communities to follow suit." On a cold winter night, almost half of the 1,000 people that live in Ashton Hayes attended the first meeting about going carbon neutral. Over hot apple pie, they began sharing ideas about how to fight climate change in their own community.

After calculating how much carbon dioxide the town emitted (about 4765.76 tons per year), they decided to create a "carbon sink" of trees to help absorb it. They figured that they would need to plant 16,000 trees, or about 16 trees per person. They were careful to plant trees native to the area that would benefit the local ecosystem. As of December of 2006,

52

 http://www.goingcarbonneutral.co.uk *Visit Ashton Hayes.*

Entering Ashton Hayes.

the townspeople had planted more than 5,500 trees.

Residents of Ashton Hayes are now working to create their own micro-grid of green energy from renewable sources. This would mean that all the electricity they received would come from renewable energy sources like wind and sun. In addition, they are growing elephant grass to use for fuel and providing free eco-driving classes.

Ashton Hayes families and local businesses have made changes in their homes and buildings as well. Alan and Sheila Ryder found that just by converting to energy-efficient lightbulbs they reduced their electricity use at

An energy-efficient fluorescent lightbulb.

home by about half. The Golden Lion pub is switching to renewable energy sources, such as solar, for its electricity. It is also composting, turning off appliances at night, and buying locally grown food.

Ashton Hayes schoolchildren wrote and sang a carbon-neutral rap song, featured in a short DVD film about Ashton Hayes (available on their website at http://www.goingcarbonneutral.co.uk/).

The town of Ashton Hayes.

action: Analyze This Quote

The famous race car driver Mario Andretti said, "Failure is success if we learn from it." Do you agree with him? Why or why not? What kinds of things do you think people can learn from the failure of climate change? Name some ways we could turn our failure into success.

Student teams discuss the quote and write down their ideas for turning climate change failure into success. Teams share their thoughts with the class.

53

Roots & Shoots Grows Young Environmentalists

Roots & Shoots (http://www.roots andshoots.org) is a program of the Jane Goodall Institute, a group founded by **primatologist,** environmentalist, and humanitarian Jane Goodall. Roots & Shoots is a network of groups of young people working to help animals and the environment in almost 100 countries around the world. Roots & Shoots kids and teens have worked with adults in schools and communities on projects ranging from protecting wildlife to starting recycling programs to educating people.

Roots & Shoots youth groups raised $50,000 to help orphaned chimpanzees whose parents had been killed by poachers in the Republic of Congo. Roots & Shoots youth around the world recognized the growing number of orphaned chimps and the need for a dormitory where they could be cared for. So they found creative ways to raise money to build the dormitory. They held a pet show, sold hand-made necklaces and home-grown vegetables and flowers, and convinced an insurance company to make a donation. With help from matching funds, Roots & Shoots youth met their goal. The money was then donated to Tchimpounga chimpanzee sanctuary, the largest chimpanzee sanctuary in Africa.

A Roots & Shoots group at Dewey Elementary School in Evanston, Illinois, called The Peaceweavers has done many things to help the environment in its community. Started in 2002 with 12 members, the group now has over 50 kids. The Peaceweavers have cleaned up local beaches, made bird houses, tested water samples, made quilts, flown their peace dove on Roots & Shoots Day of Peace, and much more.

A Roots & Shoots group at the Washington, D.C., Green Festival.

54

Their latest goal is to stop the use of Styrofoam lunch trays in their school. They estimated that two school districts in their area use about 4,000 styrofoam trays per day, 80,000 per month, and 960,000 per year. Through research and science experiments and with help from their teacher Pat Cleveland, the kids learned that Styrofoam (or polystyrene) is made from fossil fuel and is not recyclable. They suggested cardboard trays as a more environmentally friendly alternative. They're still waiting to find out if the school will change its policy on the lunch trays.

Roots & Shoots has teamed up with R.O.A.R. (Reach Out, Act, Respond), created by Animal Planet, a campaign to help animals around the world. Several young members of Roots & Shoots have been featured on Animal Planet. Chase Pickering, a Roots & Shoots Youth Fellow from Asheville, North Carolina, was chosen to make a promotional video for R.O.A.R. He was able to talk about the birds of prey he rescued and held up a Eurasian Eagle Owl with a 6-foot-wingspan in front of the camera.

Eurasian Eagle Owl.

Roots & Shoots

Climate Change Action Projects

Backyard Wildlife Habitat Program

The National Wildlife Federation's Backyard Wildlife Habitat program will teach you how to turn your backyard into a great place for wildlife. Find out how to get your Backyard Wildlife Certificate at http://www.nwf.org/backyard. Visit the global warming sections of their website for more ideas about what you can do to help reduce climate change.

Campus Climate Challenge

This network of youth organizations is fighting climate change by creating 100 percent clean energy policies in high schools and college campuses across Canada and the United States. Go to http://www.climatechallenge.org/home to learn more.

COOL fact

Replacing a traditional grass lawn with native trees and plants can attract a wide range of animals, such as butterflies, bees, birds, toads, salamanders, opossums, deer, and foxes.

http://www.rootsandshoots.org/kidsandteens *Get involved.*

Al Gore speaking about global warming at the University of Miami in February 2007.

Eco-Hero

Al Gore

Former U.S. Vice President and presidential nominee Al Gore (1948–) was one of the first politicians to realize the seriousness of global warming. He began writing and speaking out about it back in the 1970s and worked to pass the Kyoto Treaty in the 1990s. Today he leads the world in the effort to raise awareness about climate change. His book and Oscar-winning film *An Inconvenient Truth* are based on lectures on climate change that he gives around the world. In 2007, he organized the world-concert event Live Earth to raise awareness and money to fight climate change.

The Climate Project

Headed by Al Gore, the Climate Project is training 1,000 people across the United States to present slide shows to educate people about the information in Al Gore's book and film *An Inconvenient Truth*. Find out more by visiting http://www.theclimateproject.org.

Focus the Nation

Focus the Nation is organizing teach-ins about climate change in K-12 schools, colleges, and universities around the United States. College professors and students travel around the country to talk about climate change solutions and help kids and adults get involved. Learn more at http://www.focusthenation .org/k-12.php.

action: Sign up for Focus the Nation

Visit the Focus the Nation website to find out about events in your area that you can attend. If there are none, sign up to organize an event in your school, community, church, or business. Ask a parent, teacher, or other adult in your community to help you organize the event.

Students attend a Focus the Nation event or, if there are not any locally, they work together to design and organize one.

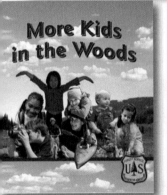

More Kids in the Woods

The U.S. Forest Service started More Kids in the Woods to inspire kids to care about nature and work to protect it. More Kids in the Woods is providing 1.5 million dollars in grants for projects that help connect kids with nature and the outdoors. Learn more about the projects they support at http://www.fs.fed.us.

1% for the Planet

Businesses that join 1% for the Planet donate 1 percent of their profits to environmental groups around the world. Visit them at http://www.onepercentfortheplanet.org.

Pew Center on Global Climate Change

This nonprofit organization works with scientists, politicians, businesspeople, journalists, and the public to identify climate change problems and create and implement practical solutions. Learn more at http://www.pewclimate.org.

The Wildlands Project

The Wildlands Project is reducing species extinctions and fostering global **biodiversity** by creating networks of interconnected land in North America where wildlife can travel safely from place to place. Learn more at http://www.twp.org.

Eileen Claussen, president of the Pew Center on Global Climate Change, at a press conference held by the United States Climate Action Partnership. USCAP is a group of businesses and environmental organizations that want the federal government to pass laws requiring the lowering of greenhouse gas emissions.

http://www.focusthenation.org/k-12.php *Focus your school.*

Rainforest Alliance

The Rainforest Alliance works to protect rainforest biodiversity by teaching people and businesses sustainable behavior and practices. Visit their education page to learn more about rainforests and how you can help: http://www.rainforest-alliance.org/programs/education/index.html.

Step It Up

Step It Up organized the first National Day of Climate Action on April 14, 2007, which included 1,400 events and rallies around the country. The goal of the events was to raise awareness about climate change and to ask Congress to cut carbon dioxide emissions 80 percent, or 2 percent a year, by 2050. Nature writer Bill McKibben and five Middlebury College students started Step It Up. Visit their website to find out what they're doing next: http://www.stepitup2007.org.

More than 1,000 middle-school students spelling out "Step It Up" in the snow in Park City, Utah.

Tree for All

The Woodland Trust's Tree For All project aims to involve one million children across the United Kingdom in planting 12 million trees over five years between 2004 and 2009. As part of the project, the Trust runs a series of events throughout the tree planting season, provides free Internet learning resources and information on planting trees, and offers free hedge and woodland packs for schools and youth groups. For more information visit http://www.treeforall.org.uk.

http://www.stepitup2007.org/signup *Start an action.*

Trees for the Future

Trees for the Future has been organizing tree planting projects around the world since the early 1970s. Their goal is to restore trees and forests to areas of the world that have been degraded by deforestation. Today they have planting programs in parts of Africa, Asia, Latin America, and North America. Learn more about them and how you can get involved at http://www.treesftf.org/main.htm.

Union of Concerned Scientists

The Union of Concerned Scientists is a group of respected scientists around the world who work to understand environmental problems and create solutions to those problems. They help educate politicians, journalists, businesses, and individual citizens to protect the earth and reduce climate change. Learn more at http://www.ucsusa.org/.

COOL fact

Roads and highways crisscross wildlife habitat around the world, making it dangerous for animals to move around. Cars kill about one million animals in the United States each day. Defenders of Wildlife is working to reduce animal deaths by providing safe wildlife crossings, such as elk underpasses and "toad tunnels."

action: Read "Warning to Humanity"

Back in 1992 the Union of Concerned Scientists, including many Nobel Prize winners from around the world, published "World Scientists' Warning to Humanity." They asked citizens of the world to make changes such as replacing fossil fuels with renewable energy sources, protecting wildlife, and securing equality for women. Their warning is even more urgent today than it was then. Find out what else they said at http://www.actionbioscience.org/environment/worldscientists.html.

Students read "Warning to Humanity" together as a class and discuss why it is even more urgent today than when it was written.

Chapter Summary

People around the world are working hard to reduce climate change. The village of Ashton Hayes is the first town in England trying to become carbon neutral. Roots & Shoots is helping kids work together to fight climate change and its effects in their schools and communities. Other organizations are fighting climate change through education, tree planting, backyard habitat projects, and more.

6 How You Can Help Fight Climate Change

*Pretty much all the honest truthtelling
there is in the world is done by children.*
—Oliver Wendell Holmes

*No person is your friend who demands
your silence, or denies your right to grow.*
—Alice Walker

Climate change and its effects are making many people feel afraid. People do different things when they are afraid. Some pretend they are not afraid and that there is nothing to be afraid of. They ignore the problem and do nothing until it is too late. Other people get very upset and feel they cannot do anything to solve the problem. They give up. But there are always smart and brave people who see that there is a problem and look for ways to solve it. These people might feel afraid, but they don't let their fear stop them from taking action.

Sunrise over the Mediterranean Sea.

Throughout history people have accomplished many amazing things. We have made tools, invented written language, founded democratic government, cured diseases, discovered electricity, built roads and bridges, outlawed slavery, invented computers, established public education, visited the moon, and created the Internet. We take many of these things for granted now, but before they happened each of these accomplishments probably seemed as difficult to people of earlier times as solving climate change does to us now.

It is easy to think that your own small concerns are the most important things in the world. It is easy to worry about how your hair looks, whether people like you, who will win the game, what grade you will get, or whose joke is funniest. But, really, the most important thing in life is life. Without life there is nothing. Life around you—trees, birds, earthworms, animals, flowers, family and friends, classmates and teachers—these are what matter most. All life needs fresh air, clean water, and healthy land where things can grow. Without a healthy environment, living things cannot survive.

It is not too late to make things better for our planet, ourselves, and all the other living things here on Earth. There is nothing more important than taking care of our home. It is the only home we have, and as far as we know the only place in the universe where there is life.

Change Your Thinking

action: Replace Fear with Solutions

Write down five things about climate change that scare you. Then write down possible solutions to the things that scare you. Share your thoughts with a friend or family member. Find out how climate change makes that person feel and talk about solutions together.

Students work in teams of three or four to share their fears and ideas for possible solutions. Then each team creates a chart of its fears and solutions to display in the classroom.

A good way to start to make things better is to change the way you think about your life and the world around you. Here are some changes you can make in your own thinking:

Old Negative Thinking	New Positive Thinking
People are not animals.	Humans are a type of animal called a mammal.
People are better than animals.	Animals are as important as people.
People are smarter than animals.	All living things are intelligent in different ways.
The way I live doesn't affect anyone.	The way I live affects the world around me.
I don't want to change the way I do things.	I want to change the way I live to help the earth.
The earth is so big I can't change it.	I can help make the world a better place.
The earth is so big people can't hurt it.	There are so many of us now, we need to be careful with the earth.
I only care about my own life.	I care about all living things.
Nature is separate from me.	I am part of nature.
It doesn't matter what I do.	What I do is important and affects others.
My life is small and unimportant.	I am a part of the world, and I matter.
The future doesn't matter.	I want to live a good life and maybe have a family some day.
It is too late to do anything.	There is time to make things better now and in the future.
I don't know how to help.	I want to learn how I can help.
I am not good at things.	Everyone is good at something, and so am I.
Life on earth is ruined.	Life is powerful and always finds ways to renew itself.
People only care about themselves.	Many people care about the world and work to make it better.

This New Jersey elementary school Earth Day display encourages kids to take a hands-on approach to the earth's problems.

Don't Think of Yourself as a Consumer

You've probably heard the word *consumer*. Often business people call their customers consumers. To *consume* means "to eat or use up." To call people consumers is like saying all we do is eat and use things up.

All living things must consume to survive, but all living things give back too. Everything consumes and everything is consumed. Plants consume sunlight and nutrients from the soil and then die and make more soil for more plants. Shellfish consume plankton, and then birds eat shellfish. Small animals consume insects, and then big animals consume small animals. Big animals die, and bacteria consume their bodies and make soil again. Life becomes food for others types of life.

Life also creates new life. Trees make seeds that make more trees. Animals have babies, or offspring. And those offspring in turn have their own offspring. All life is about consuming and creating, taking and giving. In our own lives we give and take love, food, conversation, help, and other things we need.

If everyone gave back as much as they took, everyone would have enough of what they need. However, when people take more than they need and give less than they take, there is an imbalance. Somewhere, someone will not have enough.

Identify Your Strengths

We are all born with strengths, or things we are good at and like to do. Some of us are good talkers, good athletes, good teachers, or good planners. Others are

action: Give More, Take Less

Think of three ways you can take less and three ways you can give more in your life. Create a chart of your "give-more goals" and "take-less goals" and how you plan to achieve them. Then track your progress on the chart. You might also want to challenge each of your family members to think of ways they can take less and give more in their lives. Make a chart of each family member's "give-more goals" and "take-less goals" and track how each person achieves them.

The class creates a master chart and each student tracks his or her progress on the chart each week.

More than 150 5-foot globes on the topic of climate change were on display in Chicago over the summer of 2007. Each globe highlighted a different climate change problem and solution.

The best way for you to fight climate change is to use your own strengths to do it. If you like to write, then write about climate change. If you like to teach, teach others about climate change. If you like to organize groups, start a group to fight climate change. If you like to take care of animals, volunteer at an animal shelter or adopt an animal that needs a home (with permission from your

good at writing, making people laugh, fixing things, cooking, farming, singing, making decisions, or taking care of children or animals. Still others like to invent new things or ideas, study the world around them, or travel to new places.

This roof garden is on the top of the Chicago City Hall building.

action: What Are Your Strengths?

Here are some questions to ask yourself about your strengths. Write down your answers. Then use them to think about things you can do to fight climate change. Share your ideas with a friend or family member to see what he or she thinks.

- What are you good at?
- What makes you feel proud of yourself?
- What do you like about yourself?
- What do others like about you?
- What do you like to do?
- What do you care about?
- What things would you like to change in the world?
- When have you had the most fun in your life?
- What kinds of people do you admire and why?
- What are your friends like?
- What do your friends care about?

Students work in pairs to discuss and record their strengths. They work together to come up with ideas for how they can best use their strengths to fight climate change. Then they help each other make action plans for implementing their ideas.

A volunteer planting a tree in the Sierra Mountains in an area damaged by logging and gold mining. Volunteers planted 2,000 trees to reforest the area and help offset the carbon emissions from the bonfires at the Burning Man Festival.

family!). If you are interested in film, make a movie about climate change. There is no single right way to help Earth. Things will get better in countless ways by countless people making countless changes. You will help the most by doing what you care about most, because that is what you will do best and with the most passion.

Change Your Life: What You and Your Family Can Do

Computer recycling, Ann Arbor, Michigan.

Grass roots change. Change from the ground up. The small things in life matter most. Change begins at home. You've probably heard some of these expressions. They all add up to the same idea, which is that individual actions make a difference. There are many things you and your family can do to help reduce climate change and make your home planet a healthier place for all living things. From **conserving** energy to helping wildlife, get started today!

BYO (Bring Your Own)

- Bring your own reusable bags when you go shopping.
- Bring your own reusable cup when you have coffee, tea, or other drinks.
- Bring your own refillable water bottle.

Conserve

- Don't leave water running when you're washing dishes or brushing your teeth.
- Install low-flow shower heads and toilets.

- Do only full laundry and dishwasher loads.
- Turn off the dishwasher drying cycle.
- Substitute cold water for hot.
- Take shorter and fewer showers.
- Don't water your lawn. If you must, do it at night so it won't evaporate in the sun.
- Use a push mower.

Hanging laundry to dry reduces carbon emissions.

- Insulate your house to conserve heat and air conditioning.
- Install double-pane windows for insulation.
- Keep your furnace filter clean so it runs efficiently.
- Keep your refrigerator coils clean so it runs efficiently.
- Keep your heat and AC low or off when you are not home and/or sleeping.
- Line dry your clothes.
- Cover pots when you cook.
- Keep your car tires fully inflated.

- Get off junk mail lists.
- Do online banking and bill paying to reduce paper use.
- Use a ceiling fan to help distribute your heat and air conditioning.
- Don't buy bottled water. Use a reusable water bottle instead.

action: Junk Your Junk Mail

Each year millions of trees are cut down and billions of gallons of water are used to make junk mail. A great way to save trees, conserve water, and reduce waste in landfills is to stop receiving junk mail. Find out how to stop your junk mail at the Junk Mail Reduction Kit page of the Center for the Development of Recycling: http://www.recyclestuff.org/JunkMail.asp.

Student teams do online research to find statistics about junk-mail waste. They also visit the website to learn how to stop junk mail. Then they create a letter to their parents explaining why they should stop junk mail at home and how to do it. Teams share their letters with the class, revise them based on their shared ideas, and then take them home to show their parents.

Park It

- Walk and/or ride your bike instead of drive.
- Take public transportation instead of drive.
- Carpool.
- Work at home.
- Combine errands.

Free recycling bins at the Athens, Ohio, Earth Day 5K Race to Recycle.

Dragon made from plastic bags, aluminum foil, and aluminum cans in the Paris, France, Zoological Park.

Reduce, Reuse, Recycle

- Compost your leftovers and use the compost for gardening.
- Compost (don't burn) leaves and yard waste.

- Use less, buy less, reuse, repair, borrow, and share as much as you can. Buy and sell used stuff through places like freecycle.org, craigslist.org, and eBay.com.
- Recycle as much as you can, including glass, metals, paper, plastic, and cardboard.
- Recycle your old cell phones.

U.S. Waste Statistics

- Enough hazardous waste is produced each year to fill the New Orleans Superdome 1,500 times over.
- 900 million trees are cut down each year to make paper.
- About one-third of waste is from packaging.
- Improperly dumped car oil pollutes our environment each year with 16 times the amount of pollution created by the Exxon Valdez oil spill.

U.S. Recycling Statistics

- 1,500 aluminum cans are recycled every second.
- It takes 90 percent less energy to recycle an aluminum can than to produce a new one.
- Making recycled white paper uses 75 less energy and produces 74 percent less air pollution and 35 percent less water pollution than making new paper.
- Recycling 1 ton of cardboard saves over 9 cubic yards of landfill space.

http://www.freecycle.org *Don't toss it. Freecycle it!*

action: Waste Not

The average person in the United States produces 56 tons of trash each year. Assuming you make an average amount of garbage, calculate how many pounds of trash you have created in your lifetime (2,000 pounds = 1 ton). Then calculate how much trash your family members have created in their lifetimes. Learn about how to reduce the amount of garbage you and your family create by visiting http://www.reduce.org.

After calculating their individual trash production, students work together to calculate the trash production of the whole class. Then they form six teams and research how to reduce waste in the following areas discussed on the website: at home, in school, in the yard, at the holidays, while traveling, and while shopping. Teams report their findings to the class. Then they collaborate on a Trash Reduction Guide with tips to share with their families and the rest of the school.

action: Help Gorillas by Recycling Old Cell Phones

Cell phones are made with a mineral called coltan, which is mined from the African forests of Congo. Coltan mining is destroying habitat for endangered gorillas and other wildlife that live in Congo. Mining activities in Congo also have increased **poaching**, or illegal hunting, of gorillas. Recycling cell phones can stop the need for more coltan mining and help Congo wildlife. Find out how you can recycle your old cell phones at http://www.eco-cell.org/. Tell everyone you know to do the same!

Students work together to organize a cell phone recycling program in the school. They find out where to send the old cell phones by visiting the website and set up a school drop off location for the cell phones. They advertise the program by creating and displaying posters explaining the program details and how recycling can help Congo gorillas.

Shop Smart

- Avoid buying things made of plastic or with plastic packaging unless it is recycled.
- Buy recycled paper products.
- Use cloth napkins and towels instead of paper.
- Buy wood that has been reclaimed or that has been grown in a sustainably managed forest.
- Change your old incandescent lightbulbs to fluorescents.
- Buy locally grown food.
- Buy organic food.

 http://www.reduce.org *Reduce trash at school.*

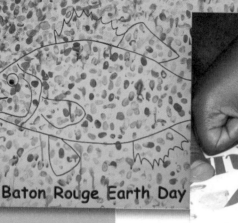

I pledge to help take care of the wetlands:

Baton Rouge Earth Day

By putting their thumbprints on this poster, children at the 2007 Baton Rouge Earth Day celebration pledge to take care of the wetlands.

Support Wildlife

- Plant native trees, bushes, and flowers in your yard and/or community instead of grass to support wildlife and cool and **oxygenate** the atmosphere.
- Plant a garden and grow your own food.
- Create animal habitat in your yard: bird houses and feeders, a pond or bird bath, bat boxes, flowering and fruiting trees and bushes, snags (dead trees), logs, piles of yard debris, and so on.

- Buy organic clothing and clothing made from sustainable fabrics such as hemp and bamboo.
- Eat more vegetables and fruit and less or no meat.
- Shop close to home.
- Buy shade-grown, fair-trade coffee.
- Buy sustainably caught seafood.
- Buy in-season produce.

Downy woodpeckers stopping for a bite.

Spread the Word

- Tell your friends, classmates, and relatives about climate change and what they can do to help stop it.

Organic carrots are healthier to grow and eat.

- Treat animals with respect. Leave them alone. Don't go near nests or dens. Be quiet in the woods and other places that are home to wildlife.

Take Political Action

- Find out if your town has agreed to the Kyoto Treaty guidelines. If it hasn't, contact your mayor and urge him or her to do so.
- Vote for politicians who support our environment.
- Write or email your representatives in Congress and ask them to work to reduce climate change.
- Join or support environmental organizations.

Playing soccer is fun and healthy, and it doesn't release carbon dioxide.

Turn It off

- Turn off lights and other appliances when not in use.
- Unplug appliances when not in use. Even when switched off, they drain a lot of electricity. For convenience, plug them into a power strip that you can switch off.
- Don't idle the car.
- Spend more time doing energy-free things, like reading, walking, playing games, or hanging out with friends.

Use Nontoxic Products

- Use natural cleaners in your home.
- Use natural fertilizers and pest control methods in your yard and garden.
- Buy **nontoxic** household products (e.g., nontoxic paints, flooring, carpet, and bedding).

action: Turn on, Turn off

Here is a good rule of thumb to follow: Whenever you turn something on, turn something else off. For example, if you turn on a fan, turn off the radio. Or if you turn on a light, turn off a different one. You may not always be able to do this, but you'll be surprised how often you can.

Students work in teams to develop plans for offsetting energy use and carbon emissions at school. For example, they might decide to plant trees to offset the school furnace emissions. Teams share their ideas, and the class develops a few of the ideas together and makes a plan for implementing them at school.

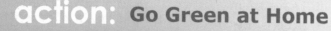

action: Go Green at Home

Chances are your home contains environmentally harmful chemicals that could be replaced with safe, nontoxic alternatives. Look at the cleaning, gardening, and household repair products around your home. Talk with your parents about replacing these items. Contact your local county health department to find out how to safely dispose of them. Look for eco-friendly alternatives at your local natural food or home store. You can also make your own natural cleaners with common ingredients such as lemon juice, white wine vinegar, and baking soda. Learn more at the Toxics at Home page of http://www.reduce.org.

Teams choose different sections of the Toxics at Home page of the website. Teams research their assigned areas and then work together to create a Green Home Catalog to take home to help educate their families.

Instead of throwing away this damaged shower curtain, the owner used a piece of metal can and a rivet gun to fix it.

A poster for a community Earth Day ivy pull.

Use Renewable Energy

- Use solar panels or wind turbines.
- Sign up to receive electricity through your power company from renewable energy sources.
- Drive a hybrid car or convert your car to biofuel.
- Invest in green energy.

Think Bigger

Making small changes in your lifestyle is very important. If lots and lots of people make these changes, it will make a big difference. But small changes are not enough. Don't be afraid to think big. Here are some ways you can do even more. See if your family, friends, teachers, or neighbors would like to get involved too. The more people you can get to help, the more it will help the earth. Look at the list of suggestions here. You can also visit the websites of the great organizations mentioned in Chapter 5 to get involved in climate change action groups.

- Start your own environmental magazine, online journal, or blog.
- Organize an Earth Day event in your neighborhood: pick up garbage, plant trees, restore a stream, remove ivy or other damaging plants, or start a

community garden.

- Volunteer at an animal shelter or environmental organization.
- Start a repair business to help fix things for people so they don't throw them away.
- Organize a cleanup day at a local park or beach.
- Start a recycling program at school or in your community.
- Organize a carpool.
- Create a walk-to-school or ride-to-school group.
- Start a climate change education campaign to teach people about climate change problems and solutions in your school or community.
- Invent an alternative form of energy for the world.

Above: This company-based cleanup crew cleaned up a mile of beach, filling 10 garbage bags. Below: A community garden in Pittsburgh, Pennsylvania.

Young volunteers helping to promote homeless animal adoption as part of the Mayor's Alliance for New York City's Animals.

Chapter Summary

The first steps to taking action against climate change are to overcome your fear, change your thinking, identify your strengths, and start changing your life. There are many lifestyle changes that you and your family can make to help reduce climate change and its effects: drive less, reduce your use of electricity, conserve resources like water and paper, help wildlife, switch to renewable energy, reduce, reuse, recycle, spread the word about climate change, shop responsibly, and take political action. But don't stop with these changes. Use your creativity and strengths to do something even bigger and bolder to help.

7 Get Started!

> How wonderful it is that nobody need wait a single moment before starting to improve the world.
> —Anne Frank

> A journey of a thousand miles begins with a single step.
> —Confucius

Iceberg in Tracy Arm, Alaska.

A young activist protests oil drilling in the Alaskan Wildlife Refuge.

We've talked about many things people are doing that are changing Earth's atmosphere and harming living things. There is an imbalance in Earth's climate, an imbalance between people and other life forms, and an imbalance among people of the world. People's machines are putting too much carbon dioxide into the atmosphere, causing our world to heat up and our environment to change. People are taking too much land, water, and food and leaving too little for other animals and plant life. And people in some parts of the world have more than they need, while other people have too little.

These imbalances are causing problems that are affecting life everywhere. The weather is changing, animals are going extinct, wilderness areas are shrinking, and people are starving or dying of diseases that could be prevented. But as we have discussed in this book there are solutions to these problems. We do not have to continue to make these problems worse. We have an opportunity to make our world a better place for all living things, and we need to start now.

72

action: Your Next Steps

You may already have taken steps at home or school to fight climate change. What can you do next? Make a chart of your climate action goals. Record what you've already done, what you want to do right away, and what you hope to do in the future. Refer to your chart from time to time to track your progress.

Students work together to create a chart of climate action goals for the whole class. They track their progress together regularly.

A volunteer for the Earth Conservation Corps speaks with visitors at the Washington, D.C., Green Festival.

You Can Do It!

Kids sometimes find it difficult to understand the complicated ways the world works. Just remember that adults also feel that they don't understand everything and can't control everything. The world is too big and complex for any one person to be able to know or do it all. But this doesn't mean that your life is unimportant or that you can't make a difference in the world. Whether you are 8 or 80, you have an important place in the world, and you have a responsibility as a citizen of Earth.

Even the bravest, smartest, strongest people feel afraid and discouraged sometimes. If you feel scared or discouraged, it is normal. The best way to stop feeling that way is to take action. Take the suggestions in this book and start making changes in your own life. Talk with your family about how all of you can fight climate change and help the earth. Then talk to your friends, teachers, classmates, relatives, and neighbors. Tell them what you have learned and why it is important for all of us to change the way we think and live.

Respect yourself, other living things, and your home planet. Do everything you can to make our world a good, positive, healthy place for all to live. Whether you pick up trash at the park or invent a new source of renewable energy, your actions have an effect on the world. Your faith in the future and your respect and love for life are your greatest strengths. Use these strengths as you work to fix climate change. If people, young and old, work together, we can reduce the causes and effects of climate change and make our amazing home planet Earth a healthier, happier place for all living things. Good living and good luck!

Chapter Summary

The way many people live has changed Earth's climate and created other dangerous imbalances for life everywhere. Climate change and other related problems can be scary and overwhelming. Even adults feel overwhelmed at times. But by believing in yourself, in the power of life itself, and in the future, you can be the change you wish to see in the world.

Terms

Adaptation Genetic change in response to the environment.

Agricultural chemicals Pesticides and fertilizers used in farming.

Anthropogenic Caused by humans.

Aquatic Growing or living in water.

Aquifer An underground layer of rock or sand that contains water.

Arid Too dry to grow crops.

Atmosphere The layer of gases that surrounds Earth, keeping it warm and supporting life.

Biodegrade To break down into small harmless parts by the action of living things.

Biodiversity The variety of species living in an environment, making it healthy.

Carbon dioxide An odorless gas that is produced when fossil fuels are burned, when animals breathe, and when plants or animals decay.

Carbon monoxide A poisonous gas, or pollution, released by car engines and factories.

Carbon neutral A condition in which carbon dioxide emissions have been offset by things that absorb carbon dioxide, such as planting trees, so there is no overall addition of carbon dioxide to the atmposhere.

Climate Weather (temperature, wind, precipitation, and ocean currents) patterns over time.

Climate change Change to Earth's weather and environment as a result of increased global temperatures from increased carbon dioxide in Earth's atmosphere trapping more heat from the sun.

Climate change action Lifestyle and societal changes that help reduce the causes and effects of climate change.

Composting Allowing leftover food and yard waste to decay naturally back into the soil.

Conservation Protecting and carefully managing natural resources like water and forests so they are not damaged or destroyed.

Conserve To keep safe and not use up or waste.

Coral Small ocean animals that secrete and live in hard limestone skeletons.

Coral bleaching A condition in which coral dies and loses its color. Warmer ocean temperatures and pollution are two causes of coral bleaching.

Coral reef A rich plant and animal habitat in and around coral formations in the ocean.

Decade Ten years.

Deforestation Cutting down forest areas and destroying the entire forest ecosystem.

Ecosystem An interconnected community of living things and their environment.

Emission A substance given off into the air.

Endangered species A type of living thing threatened with extinction usually because of environmental changes such as habitat loss, disease, hunting, pollution, or global warming.

Erode To wear away from the action of wind, rain, or glacial ice.

Evolution Change in living things over time in response to environmental conditions.

Extinct species A type of living thing that no longer exists on Earth.

Fertile Able to make or support life.

Fossil fuels Coal, oil, and natural gas extracted from the earth. They are called *fossil* fuels, because they formed in the earth over millions of years.

Genetic Having to do with genes in a living thing that control its traits, such as coloring or intelligence.

Global warming Warming on Earth, currently from increased carbon dioxide gas in the atmosphere (caused by humans burning fossil fuels) trapping more of the sun's heat.

Greenhouse gases The gases in Earth's atmosphere that hold in the sun's heat and support life.

Glacier A large, thick body of ice.

Habitat A place where a species lives and grows.

Hemisphere Half of Earth's spherical body.

Hydropower Energy generated from moving water.

Incentive Something, like a law, that motivates or produces action or change.

Mass extinction An event on Earth in which half or more of all species die off.

Megafauna Large animals, such as giant beavers, that once lived on Earth.

Microorganism A living thing too small to be seen without a microscope.

Multicellular Having more than one cell.

Native species Species that originally lived in and are adapted to a particular place.

Nitrogen A gas that makes up 78 percent of Earth's atmosphere and helps form living tissue.

Nontoxic Safe, nonpoisonous.

Organism A living thing.

Overpopulation The condition of so many members of a species living in a place that it harms the environment and quality of life and may lead to population crash.

Oxygen A gas that makes up 21 percent of Earth's atmosphere and is present in elements such as water, rock, and living things.

Oxygenate To provide with oxygen.

Phytoplankton Tiny, floating plantlife that live in water.

Poaching The illegal hunting of animals.

Population The number of members of a species in a specific place.

Precipitation An element of Earth's climate in the form of rain, snow, or hail.

Recycle To reuse something or change something so it can be used again for another purpose.

Renewable energy Energy that can be replaced by natural ecological cycles.

Solar energy Energy from the sun.

Species A type of living thing, such as a fiddler crab, Japanese maple, or red squirrel.

Sustainable A way of doing something so that it can be continued, without damaging or destroying living things, ecosystems, or the environment.

Temperate Mild, or not having extremes.

Thermohaline circulation The largest ocean current on Earth, which helps regulate the climate.

Toxic Poisonous.

Tropical From a region on Earth where there is no frost and so there is year-round plant growth.

Wind power Energy from the wind, usually captured in wind turbines.

Resources

More Great Nonprofit Groups

The American Society for the Prevention of Cruelty to Animals, http://www.aspca.org/
Blue Ocean Institute, http://www.blueocean.org
Care2 Connect, http://www.passport.care2.net
Center for Biological Diversity, http://www.biologicaldiversity.org
Conservation Northwest, http://www.conservationnw.org
Defenders of Wildlife, http://www.defenders.org
Defenders of Wildlife Kids Planet, http://www.kidsplanet.org
Envirolink, http://www.envirolink.org
Environmental Defense, http://www.environmentaldefense.org
Greenpeace, http://www.greenpeace.org
Humane Society of the United States, http://www.hsus.org
National Audubon Society, http://www.audubon.org
Natural Resources Defense Council, http://www.nrdc.org
The Nature Conservancy, http://www.nature.org
Sierra Club, http://www.sierraclub.org
Worldwatch Institute, http://worldwatch.org
World Wildlife Fund, http://www.worldwildlife.org
World Society for the Protection of Animals (WSPA), http://www.wspa.org.au/
Youth Environmental Network, http://www.orgs.takingitglobal.org/2758

Online Green Information

Grinningplanet.com, http://www.grinningplanet.com/index.htm

Idealbite, http://www.idealbite.com
Kexp.org, http://www.kexp.org/about/psa/globalwarming.asp
Treehugger, http://treehugger.com
Worldchanging, http://www.worldchanging.com

Books

Adventures of Riley eco-adventure books
An Inconvenient Truth, by Al Gore
Low-Carbon Diet, by David Gershon
Worldchanging: A User's Guide for the 21st Century, edited by Alex Steffen

Magazines

Audubon Magazine, http://www.magazine.audubon.org/
Earth First! http://www.earthfirstjournal.com
E/The Environmental Magazine, http://www.emagazine.com
Grist, http://www.grist.org
Mother Jones, http://www.motherjones.com
National Wildlife, http://www.nwf.org/nationalwildlife/
Orion, http://www.oriononline.org
Sierra Magazine, http://www.sierraclub.org/sierra/
Utne, http://www.utne.com
Yes! A Journal of Positive Futures, http://www.futurenet.org/

Movies

Grinning Planet's comprehensive list of environmental movies, http://www.grinningplanet.com/6001/environmental-movies.htm

Sources

Introduction

Louv, Richard. *Last Child in the Woods: Saving Our Children from Nature-Deficit Disorder.* Chapel Hill, NC: Algonquin Books of Chapel Hill, 2006.

Chapter 1

Brennan, Richard P. *Dictionary of Scientific Literacy.* New York: John Wiley & Sons, 1992.

Spokes, Lucinda. "Consequenes of Global Warming on Ocean Circulation." Environmental Sciences, University of East Anglia, Norwich, U.K., 2003. http://www.atmosphere.mpg.de/enid/1vr.html

Dorritie, Dan. *Killer in Our Midst: Methane Catastrophes in Earth's Past . . . and Near Future?* 2007. http://www.dcn.davis.ca.us/go/dorritie

Wikipedia. "Extremes on Earth." Updated August 8, 2007. http://www.en.wikipedia.org/wiki/Extremes_on_Earth

Kolbert, Elizabeth. *Field Notes from a Catastrophe: Man, Nature, and Climate Change.* New York: Bloomsbury Publishing, 2006.

McLean, Dewey M. "A Climate Change Mammalian Population Collapse Mechanism." 1995. http://www.filebox.vt.edu/artsci/geology/mclean/Dinosaur_Volcano_Extinction/

Pringle, Heather. "Did a Comet Wipe Out Prehistoric Americans?" *NewScientist*, May 2007. http://www.newscientist.com

United States Department of Agriculture Natural Resources Conservation Service. "The Scoop on Soil." http://www.urbantext.uiuc.edu/soil/index.html (accessed June 2007)

Chapter 2

Swenson, May. *Nature: Poems Old and New.* From "Weather." Boston: Houghton Mifflin Company, 1994.

Gore, Al. *An Inconvenient Truth: The Planetary Emergency of Global Warming and What We Can Do About It.* New York: Melcher Media, 2006.

Steffen, Alex, ed. *Worldchanging: A User's Guide for the 21st Century.* New York: Abrams, 2006.

The Soil Association. "The Importance of Soil." **http://www.soilassociation.org** (accessed June 2007)

Western Ag Innovations. "A Brief Introduction to the Importance of Soil in Ecology." http://www.westernag.ca (accessed June 2007)

Enchantedlearning.com. "Soil Layers." http://www.enchantedlearning.com/geology/soil (accessed July 2007)

Anthoni, J. Floor. "Soil Geology." 2000. http://www.seafriends.org.nz/enviro/soil/geosoil.htm

Brennan, Richard P. *Dictionary of Scientific Literacy.* New York: John Wiley & Sons, 1992.

Evans, Jo. *Ultimate Visual Dictionary.* London: DK Publishing, 2006.

Trenberth, Kevin E. "Warmer Oceans, Stronger Hurricanes." *Scientific American*, July 2007.

Offenheiser, Raymond C. *Oxfam America* email newsletter. August 8, 2007.

O'Connor, Anahad, and Graham Bowley. "Tornado Hits Brooklyn; Subway Back in Service." *The New York Times*, August 8, 2007.

Water Directors of the European Union. "Best Practices on Flood Prevention, Protection, and Mitigation." June 2003. http://floods.org/PDF/Intl_BestPractices_EU_2004.pdf

Intergovernmental Panel on Climate Change. "Fourth Assessment Report: Climate Change 2007: Climate Change Impacts, Adaptation, and Vulnerability." http://www.ipcc.ch/ (accessed May 2007)

Baez, John. "Extinction." April 8, 2006. http://math.ucr.edu/home/baez/extinction

University of California Museum of Paleontology. "Tour of Geologic Time." http://ucmp.berkeley.edu/exhibits/geologictime.php (accessed July 2007)

Chicago Field Museum. "Evolving Planet Exhibit: Tour Through Time." 2007. http://www.fieldmuseum.org/evolvingplanet/exhibition.asp

Hutzler, Charles. "Ancient Species of Dolphin Believed Extinct." *The Associated Press*, December 14, 2006.

Stein, Sharyn. "Environmental Defense Joins Interior Secretary to Celebrate American Bald Eagle's Removal From Endangered Species List." June 28, 2007. http://www.environmentaldefense.org/pressrelease.cfm?ContentID=6578

U.S. Fish & Wildlife Service Endangered Species Program. Updated August 8, 2007. http://www.fws.gov/endangered/

Kolbert, Elizabeth. "Stung: The Mysterious Decline of the Honeybee." *The New Yorker*, August 6, 2007.

Wikipedia. "Coral Reef." Updated August 24, 2007. http://www.en.wikipedia.org/wiki/Coral_reef

Wikipedia. "Coral Bleaching." Updated August 14, 2007. http://www.en.wikipedia.org/wiki/Coral_bleaching

Buchheim, Jason. "Coral Reef Bleaching." 1998. http://www.marinebiology.org/coralbleaching.htm

Kolbert, Elizabeth. *Field Notes from a Catastrophe: Man, Nature, and Climate Change*. New York: Bloomsbury Publishing, 2006.

Dorritie, Dan. *Killer in Our Midst: Methane Catastrophes in Earth's Past . . . and Near Future?* 2007. http://www.dcn.davis.ca.us/go/dorritie

Chapter 3

McKibben, Bill. *The End of Nature*. New York: Anchor Books Doubleday, 1990.

Kolbert, Elizabeth. *Field Notes from a Catastrophe: Man, Nature, and Climate Change*. New York: Bloomsbury Publishing, 2006.

Wikipedia. "Extremes on Earth." Updated August 8, 2007. http://www.en.wikipedia.org/wiki/Extremes_on_Earth

Anderson, Donald, M. "What Are Harmful Algal Blooms (HABs)?" National Oceanic and Atmospheric Administration Center for Sponsored Coastal Ocean Research. http://www.whoi.edu/redtide/whathabs/whathabs.html (accessed May 2007)

Dorritie, Dan. *Killer in Our Midst: Methane Catastrophes in Earth's Past . . . and Near Future?* 2007. http://www.dcn.davis.ca.us/go/dorritie

Gore, Al. *An Inconvenient Truth: The Planetary Emergency of Global Warming and What We Can Do About It.* New York: Melcher Media, 2006.

McKibben, Bill. *Deep Economy.* New York: Times Books Henry Holt and Company, 2007.

World Watch Institute. "Planet Gets a Lemon as Global Car Industry Revs Up." July 18, 2007.

Pollan, Michael. *Omnivore's Dilemma.* New York: Penguin Press, 2006.

Mongabay.com. "Deforestation." http://www.travel.mongabay.com/deforestation_photos.html (accessed May 2007)

Shoumatoff, Alex. "The Gasping Forest." *Vanity Fair*, May 2007.

Langewiesche, William. "Jungle Law." *Vanity Fair*, May 2007.

Seattle.Gov Office of the Mayor, Greg Nickels. "U.S. Mayors Climate Protection Agreement." http://www.seattle.gov/mayor/climate/ (accessed May 2007)

ProgressiveKid. "Go Organic: The Healthy, Responsible Choice." Updated 2005. http://www.progressivekid.com/go_organic.aspx

Mongabay.com. "Pound of Beef Produces 36 Pounds of CO2 Emissions." July 18, 2007.

Schlickeisen, Rodger. "Help on the Way for Federal Conservation?" *Defenders: The Conservation Magazine of Defenders of Wildlife*, Summer 2007.

Blue Ocean Institute. "Guide to Ocean-Friendly Seafood." Updated June 2006.

Lear, Linda. "Rachel Carson's Biography." 2007. http://www.rachelcarson.org/?v1=About

Weisman, Alan. *The World Without Us.* New York: Thomas Dunne Books St. Martin's Press, 2007.

Anup, Shah. "Poverty Facts and Stats." http://www.globalissues.org (accessed August 2007)

Bread for the World. "Hunger Facts International." http://www.bread.org (accessed August 2007)

Casey, Susan. "Plastic Ocean." *Best Life Magazine,* February 20, 2007. http://www.bestlifeonline.com/cms/publish/health-fitness/Our_oceans_are_turning_into_plastic_are_we_2.shtml (accessed October 2007)

Pala, Christopher. "No-Fishing Zones in Tropics Yield Fast Payoffs for Reefs." *The New York Times,* April 17, 2007.

Chapter 4

Noble, Craig. "California Governor Signs Historic Global Warming Law: World Watches as California Sets Standard for U.S. Action." Natural Resources Defense Council press release. September 27, 2006. http://www.nrdc.org/media/pressreleases/060927.asp

McKibben, Bill. *Deep Economy.* New York: Times Books Henry Holt and Company, 2007.

Pollan, Michael. *Omnivore's Dilemma.* New York: Penguin Press, 2006.

Ideal Bite. "If the Hamburglar Were Green, Would He Steal Big Macs?" August 1, 2007.

ProgressiveKid. "Go Organic: The Healthy, Responsible Choice." Updated 2005. http://www.progressivekid.com/go_organic.aspx

Ideal Bite. "Looking for Green in Your Own Backyard?" September 7, 2007.

Worldwatch Institute. "2006 Wind Installations Offset More Than 40 Million Tons of CO2." July 26, 2007.

Steffen, Alex, ed. *Worldchanging: A User's Guide for the 21st Century*. New York: Abrams, 2006.

Jay, Adam. "Kenyan Tree Planter Wins Peace Prize." *The Guardian*, October 8, 2004.

The Green Belt Movement. "What Is the Green Belt Movement?" October 12, 2006. http://www.greenbeltmovement.org

Chapter 5

Treehugger. "Britain to Build Five Carbon Neutral Towns." July 27, 2007.

Lazaroff, Cat. "Defenders Launches Habitat and Highways Campaign." Defenders of Wildlife press release, June 29, 2001. http://www.defenders.org

Chapter 6

Garthwaite, Josie, and Terri Trespicio. "Do Just One Thing." *Body and Soul*, May 2007.

Clean Air Council. "Waste Facts and Figures." http:// cleanair.org (accessed July 2007)

Lovgren, Stefan. "Can Cell Phone Recycling Help African Gorillas?" *National Geographic News,* January 20, 2006. http://www.news.nationalgeographic.com/news/2006/01/0120_060120_cellphones.html

Reduce.org. "Toxics at Home." http://www.reduce.org (accessed July 2007)

Acknowledgments

I am deeply grateful to the members of my advisory board for their invaluable suggestions and encouragement: Eckstein Middle School Science Teacher Jessica Levine, Breidalblik Elementary School Librarian Mary Fox, Eckstein Middle School Language Arts (and Social Studies certified) Teacher Erica Fuson, University of Washington Department of Biology Lecturer and Department of Genome Science Research Scientist Dr. Jennifer Calkins, and University of Washington Department of Genome Science Associate Professor Dr. Willie J. Swanson.

Big thank yous to Lynn Brofsky for her expert technical assistance, to Ellie Linen Low for providing a vital connection, and to sister-out-law Jill Lane for a helpful tip.

Countless thanks to my illustrator and designer extraordinaire Sarah Lane, whose vision, commitment, and resourcefulness fundamentally shaped and greatly enhanced this book.

Deepest gratitude for the enduring support of my mother Gaynette Schauer, my parent-out-laws William Lane and Dorothy Lane, and especially my father James Hall and stepmother Karen Hall whose generous support made this book possible.

And a shout out to friends and family members whose cheerleading helped keep my chin up along the way.

Photo Credits

left to right, top to bottom
(cc) *refers to the Creative Commons license. Find out more at* http://creativecommons.org/licenses/by/3.0/.

10 NASA
   NOAA
11 NOAA
12 NASA/Goddard Space Flight Center Scientific Visualization Studio 1996, http://visibleearth.nasa.gov/
   NOAA
13 NASA
   NOAA
14 (cc) Kevin Walsh, 2007
   NOAA
16 NOAA
17 NOAA
   NOAA
19 (cc) Louise Docker, 2006
20 U.S. Fish & Wildlife
22 (cc) Benjamin Stone, 2006
   (cc) Tim_Flickr, 2006
   (cc) Payton Chung, 2005
   (cc) Naadir Jeewa, 2005
23 U.S. Fish & Wildlife
24 (cc) Janice Waltzer, 2006
   (cc) Christian Guthier, 2006
   (cc) Matthew Levine, 2007
   (cc) M. Shelton, 2007
   (cc) Audrey, 2007
25 (cc) Steve & Jem Copley, 2007
   (cc) Franklin Samir, 2005
26 (cc) César Rincón, 2007

27 NASA
29 (cc) Racoles, 2007
31 (cc) Peter Kaminski, 2006
   (cc) Steve Slep, 2007
32 (cc) Benny Lin, 2006
   (cc) Jaime Haire, 2006
33 (cc) Quintus Frimschlowder III, 2006
   (cc) Allan Ferguson, 2007
34 (cc) Michael Pereckas, 2006
   (cc) Chris Brown, 2007
35 (cc) Angela Sevin, 2006
   (cc) Cory Doctorow, 2007
   (cc) View of the World, 2006
36 (cc) Jami Dwyer, 2006
   (cc) Jollence Lee, 2005
38 (cc) Bjaglin, 2007
39 (cc) Tohru Hagihara, 2007
   (cc) Concrete Forms, 2007
   (cc) Allan Ferguson, 2007
40 (cc) Richard Lyon, 2007
   (cc) Bart (Editor B), 2006
41 (cc) Mo Riza, 2006
42 (cc) Save the Wild UP, 2007
   (cc) Oliver Woodford, 2006
43 (cc) M. Prinke, 2007
44 (cc) Jim Clark, 2007
   (cc) Frank Hebbert, 2007
45 (cc) Morris K. Udall Foundation, 2007
   (cc) Joe (a.k.a. Montage Man), 2006
46 (cc) Yaffa Grinblatt, 2007
   (cc) Frank Hebbert, 2007
47 (cc) Mark Sadowski, 2007
48 (cc) Paul Heasman, 2006
   (cc) adiything, 2007
   (cc) Tobin Fricke, 2006

49 (cc) Skidrd, 2007
(cc) Seth Anderson, 2007
(cc) Audie, 2006
50 (cc) Matt Reinbold, 2006
53 (cc) Creative Photography, 2007
(cc) Dan McKay, 2006
(cc) Creative Photography, 2007
54 (cc) Aaron Logan, 2006
(cc) Ellie Van Houtte, 2006
55 (cc) Boliyou, 2006
(cc) Brian Snelson, 2006
56 (cc) Alex de Carvalho, 2007
Focus the Nation, 2007
57 Jackie Twiss, U.S. Forest Service, 2007
1% for the Planet, 2007
The Wildlands Project
(cc) World Resources Institute, 2007
58 Rainforest Alliance, 2007
Step It Up, 2007
Tree for All, 2007
Chris Pilaro/Working Films, 2007
59 Trees for the Future, 2007
Union of Concerned Scientists, 2007
60 (cc) Cat (clspeace), 2007
62 (cc) Kitty Wilkin, 2007
63 (cc) John LeGear, 2007
(cc) David Gleason, 2006, http://www
.flickr.com/photos/mind
frieze/217930564/
64 (cc) George Hotelling, 2007
(cc) Ian Baker, 2007
65 (cc) Paul Keleher, 2007
66 (cc) Sandra Nahdar, 2007
(cc) Evan (Austinevan), 2006
68 (cc) Louisiana Sea Grant College Program
of Louisiana State University, 2007

(cc) Louisiana Sea Grant College Program
of Louisiana State University, 2007
(cc) Tim Boyd, 2006
(cc) Richard Kelland, 2006
69 (cc) Masahiro Hayata, 2007
70 (cc) John (Choffee), 2005
ProgressiveKid, 2007
71 (cc) Patrick Kwan, 2006
(cc) Chris Young, 2007
(cc) Saeru, 2005
72 (cc) Jessica (WordRidden), 2005
(cc) Roger H. Goun, 2007
(cc) Ellie Van Houtte, 2006

Index

About the Author

Julie Hall is the author of numerous science and social studies curriculum books for children. Her award-winning poetry has appeared in anthologies and magazines, including *The Nation* and *The Threepenny Review.* She cofounded ProgressiveKid, a planet-friendly online company for kids and families. She is a regular contributor to *On a Ledge,* a blog about progressive parenting and green living. She lives on Bainbridge Island, Washington, where she and her partner, daughter, and rescued dogs, cats, and rabbit are happily encircled by old cedar trees.

Julie stands in front of "Planet Alert: Level Red," by Stanley Tigerman, part of a 2007 climate change exhibition in Chicago.

Green Goat Books

About Green Goat Books

The vision of Green Goat Books, the imprint of Progressive-Kid, is to support the development of progressive kids, so that the next generation will be prepared and motivated to care for our planet and its many forms of life. What's a progressive kid? We think a progressive kid is one who embodies the seven values shown at right.

Books are not for the faint of heart or head. Reading takes courage, mindfulness, receptivity, and imaginative creativity. We respect our readers and hope to challenge, inspire, and motivate them.

A tree will be planted with the purchase of every copy of this book.

http://greengoatbooks.com

Love & protect living things

Act on principle

Strive to be self-aware

Live healthfully

Honor difference

Challenge gender roles

Think creatively

Reduce,
reuse,
recycle.

Plant trees.
Support
wildlife.

Use green
modes of
transportation.

Go organic:
Grow and buy
pesticide-free.

Use
renewable
energy sources.

Change the
way you
think and live.